Contemporary
Stained Glass

Contemporary Stained Glass

A Guide to the Potential of Modern Stained Glass in Architecture

ANDREW MOOR

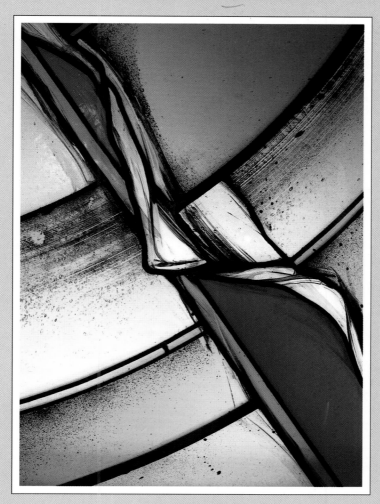

Mitchell Beazley

Contemporary Stained Glass

Andrew Moor

First published in Great Britain in 1989
by Mitchell Beazley
an imprint of Reed Consumer Books Ltd,
Michelin House, 81 Fulham Road, London SW3 6RB
and Auckland, Melbourne, Singapore and Toronto

First published in paperback 1994, reprinted 1995, 1996

Art Editor **Christopher Howson**
Editor **Robert Saxton**
Editorial Assistant **Jaspal Kharay**
Production **Ted Timberlake and Stewart Bowling**

A CIP catalogue record for this book is available from the
British Library

ISBN 1 85732 437 4

The publishers have made every effort to ensure that all
instructions given in this book are accurate and safe, but they
cannot accept liability for any resulting injury, damage or loss to
either person or property whether direct or consequential and
howsoever arising. The author and publishers will be grateful for
any information which will assist them in keeping future editions
up to date.

Typeset in ITC Garamond by Litho Link Ltd.
Colour reproduction by Scantran, Singapore
Produced by Mandarin Offset
Printed and Bound in Hong Kong

title page picture **Graham Jones,**
detail of panel,
ICI building, Millbank, London,
1988 (see page 133)

opposite, **Linda Lichtman,**
autonomous panel

pages 6-7 **Lutz Haufschild,** *Time
and Space,* panel in office lobby,
Ottawa, Canada 1989

CONTENTS

LICHTMAN '85

FOREWORD

After giving, in the course of one year, well over a hundred seminars on secular stained glass, I realized it would take most of my lifetime to show the architects of one city alone what is being done with this magical, fascinating medium. It was then that I decided to put together a book on the subject.

In recent years, amazingly few books on contemporary stained glass have come onto the market, and of these hardly any cover specifically secular work. This absence of published material has allowed the myth to continue, even in the architectural world, that stained glass is still primarily a neo-Gothic, ecclesiastical medium. This book sets out to explode that myth. It seeks to create a new image, a new sense of what stained glass is about in the modern world.

In planning the book, my aim has been to show the exciting potential of the medium, and at the same time to present the work of some of the best stained glass artists around the world. In the Portfolio sections I have focused on the work of six highly individual artists — a personal selection of talents who differ widely in style, age, experience and reputation. Elsewhere in the book I have grouped projects under thematic headings, depending on the nature of the project or the materials and techniques used.

This is a book primarily intended for the professional market — architects, designers, patrons of architecture and design. However, it is my experience that many people outside these specialist fields respond to the incomparable beauty of stained glass. For these people, too, I hope that my book will have an inspiring message.

Finally, I wish to give thanks: to Derek Dyne and John Goldsmith, without whom this project might never have taken off; to Jack Tresidder of Mitchell Beazley, who gave the book the go-ahead; to Bob Saxton, who spent many hours working with me on the text; to Christopher Howson, who designed the book and, throughout the process, increasingly came to share my enthusiasm for the medium; to Wilhelm Derix, who provided so many of the pictures; and to my wife Patrice, who first encouraged me to attempt this book and has supported me throughout.

GLASS: THE MEDIUM

Above *One of the glass blowers at the Lamberts Glass Factory in Waldsassen, W. Germany, shapes a "muff" — the term given to a cylinder of glass, before it is cut and placed back in the kiln to unfold into a piece of flat glass.*

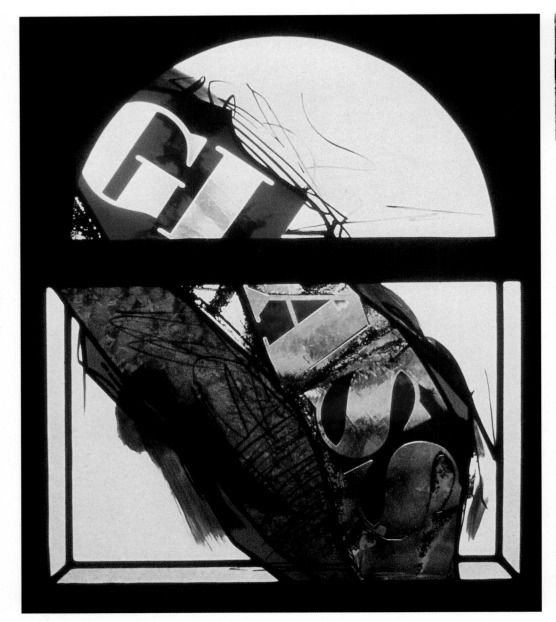

Left *Most stained glass artists will admit that the major reason they continue working in this medium is that at some point or another they fell in love with the material — mouth-blown "antique" glass. Lutz Haufschild, who created this autonomous panel in 1986, is no exception. The panel (30 x 46 in/75 x 115 cm) incorporates both etching and painting. It is a celebration of antique glass, as well as being a tribute to the German artist Johannes Schreiter. It won the Best Stained Glass Award of 1986, sponsored by the American magazine* Professional Stained Glass, *and is now part of the expanding contemporary stained glass collection at the Langen Museum, West Germany.*

It was only in the late 1950s that the British corporation Pilkington made the astounding technical breakthrough that gave us what we now call "float glass." Such a radical advance was this technique that a "state of the art" glass factory in Porz, West Germany, completed in 1972 but still unopened, was relegated to the status of a museum before it had even started production.

Float glass is virtually flawless. Its perfection is the perfection of absence. To look at a piece of float glass is to look at nothing. It is pure — perfectly flat, perfectly clear, perfectly uniform. It is the ultimate machine-made product — predictable, standardized and functional.

The medium of mouth-blown glass, on the other hand, is everything but absence: it is a presence. No two pieces are ever exactly the same. Each piece is hand-made in such a

way that its texture is unique. Mouth-blown glass has brilliance and life. It has colour that can range from the deepest, richest hues to the subtlest, palest tints. It can be of a single uniform colour, or have streaks of various colours. It can shift through a range of hues. It can be virtually transparent, or completely opaque. It can even be made up of various layers of colour on top of each other. (Virtually all stained glass is translucent, and therefore not strictly opaque. However, for ease of description we frequently use "opaque" to describe glass through which nothing can be seen.)

To employ mouth-blown glass you have to wish to make some kind of statement. A window in this material cannot simply be an aperture to the outside world: instead, the glass becomes part of the fabric and texture of the building.

Antique glass

The term "antique glass" has nothing to do with age: it is the customary label for mouth-blown flat glass. The technique may be briefly summarized as follows: Molten glass is blown up into a large bottle shape. The two ends are removed leaving a cylinder of hot glass. A vertical cut is made in the side of the cylinder, which is then placed back in the kiln. It is then folded out into a piece of flat glass.

This method goes back hundreds of years. By including various additives or performing various blowing techniques, a range of different textures and qualities are achieved.

There are five basic types of antique glass:

Plain antique

Seedy antique

Streaky antique

Reamy antique (*danziger* or water glass)

Flashed antique (simple, *opak*, opalescent or *opal*).

Glass can also be machine-rolled. The types of machine-rolled glass mainly found in stained glass designs are rolled antique, "cathedral" glass (tinted or clear), clear patterned glass (eg ribbed) and American opalescent (Tiffany).

Also used are various types of cast or bevelled glass.

Above *An example of a seedy antique glass. The small glass bubbles, which come in various densities, give the glass an opacity that can contrast well with the more transparent appearance of regular antique.*

Below *This window by California-based Peter Mollica includes a streaky antique glass, where two colours are interwoven into the material (top right). The English glassmakers Hartley Wood are renowned for this type of glass.*

Below *This domestic stained glass window reveals an interesting mixture of materials. The clear background is a* danziger *or reamy glass. Inside an outer cream border of antique seedy is a beautiful plain amber antique. The blue flower petals are executed in rolled American opalescent, and the graduated tones of the red buds are etched from a flashed glass. At the bottom of the window are three bands of "cathedral" glass.*

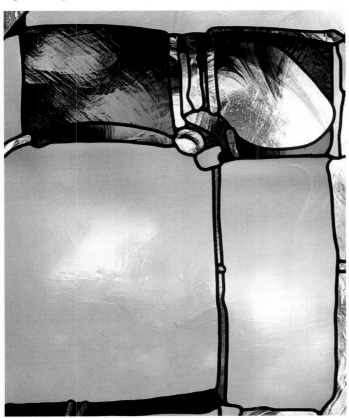

Flashed antique

COLOUR
CLEAR

A thin layer of colour is ""flashed" onto clear antique by dipping the muff into molten glass during blowing. The layer of coloured glass can be etched away completely, revealing the clear base glass, or partially, creating different intensities of the flashed colour. Both effects are shown here.

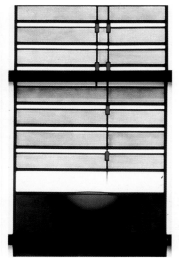

Opak

WHITE
COLOUR

A thin layer of opaque white is "flashed" onto coloured antique glass. Opak is often used for backlit panels: the white side is unattractive, and generally placed at the back, diffusing the light source. With front-lighting, opak can retain its colour well, as the light is reflected back through the colour by the white layer.

Opal

COLOUR
WHITE
CLEAR

A thin layer of transparent white flashed onto clear antique, with an additional layer of colour flashed on top. The example above (a panel by the painter Otmar Alt) shows how the colour can be etched away creating tones graduating to white. Opal glass is more pleasing from the reverse than opak, and more transparent.

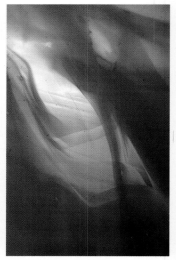

Opalescent

SHADES OF WHITE
CLEAR

A clear antique glass with a layer of transparent white flashed on top. The flashed white can come in many shades or, as in the example above, in the wispy effect characteristic of a "smoky" opalescent. Both opal and opak glass can come with a base of seedy, danziger (reamy) or regular antique glass.

"Cathedral" glass
This is a machine-rolled glass that comes in a very limited range of colours. Its title often seems rather euphemistic, as it is really tinted "lavatory" glass. The picture above shows a recently reconstructed window made in cathedral glass, with touches of American opalescent in the purple flowers.

Other machine-rolled glass
There are many other types of rolled glass — ribbed, flemish (frosted), and others. These types can be blended successfully with antique glass, as shown in the detail above from a panel by Lutz Haufschild. The glass often sparkles well and the uniformity of texture contrasts vividly with genuine antique glass.

American opalescent
This is a machine-rolled glass, developed by Tiffany in the 1870s. Few people subsequently have matched the masterpieces that Tiffany achieved in this material. It is based on an opaque white glass with streaky colour or colours weaving through. The range of colours and mixtures available is enormous.

Bevelled glass
Many artists like to use bevelled elements in their windows — as well as lenses (see pages 26-7) and prisms (page 63). These are all cast in glass, and come in clear, opal or colours. This window (by Kenneth von Roenn) also shows brilliant cutting — a technique of grinding concave shapes (in this case, circles) into the glass.

Size

Mouth-blown glass comes in two basic sizes. Most German glass comes in sheets approximately 35 x 25in (90 x 60cm). English antique glass tends to be smaller — 22 x 18in (55 x 45cm) is standard.

Rolled glass comes in much larger sizes, up to 60 x 30in (150 x 75cm). Float glass comes in larger sizes still.

Antique glass is of variable thickness, ranging from $\frac{1}{16}$ to $\frac{3}{16}$in (2-4mm), the average thickness being $\frac{1}{8}$in (3mm). Rolled and float glass, being machine-made products, come in predetermined thicknesses.

The cost factor

Antique glass is relatively expensive. The cost of the different types varies enormously: flashed glass, for example, is more expensive than regular antique. The costs of various colours also vary considerably, reds costing significantly more than other colours. Rolled glass, on the other hand, is considerably less expensive than genuine antique glass — often less than a quarter of the cost. And float glass is more economical still.

Left The central shape in this detail from Brian Clarke's "Chelsea Window" shows the varied tones that can be achieved in one single brushstroke of silverstain. Each piece in this picture has only been fired once, but with multiple firings it is possible with silverstain to achieve an even wider variety of colours and tones.

Below This small detail, taken from a work by Joachim Dorn, shows how a variety of coloured enamels can be used on glass. The quality and intensity of the colours cannot match the pure colour of glass itself, but enamels are used effectively by a number of artists. They were exploited extensively in the 18th and 19th centuries, until the Victorian Gothic Revival brought back the medieval tradition of stained glass combined with just black enamel and silverstain.

Above Different types of brush and different mixtures of paint achieve different shadings or lines on the glass. Quills, fingers or needles are often used to scratch away the initial application of paint. The picture above shows a fine example of varied brushwork by the German artist Joachim Dorn. The sole of the foot has been silverstained, and subsequently painted in black.

Above This panel by Rosalind Grimshaw shows the use of paint softening the potentially abrupt conjunctions of different coloured glasses.

Glass: the techniques

There are basically two operations that you can perform on glass. You can add to it with various types of "paint"; or you can subtract from it by etching away the surface.

Additive techniques

The primary "black" paint used for decorating glass is a dark-brown vitreous enamel. This is basically a finely ground iron oxide, mixed with powdered glass and borax. When "fired" in the kiln, the paint fuses with the surface of the glass, creating an opaque stain.

Many techniques of painting are employed, mainly with the intention of creating various degrees of translucence, or "half-tones," filtering the light through the glass. As in printing or drawing, the end-result will be a mixture of the paint, and the base medium (in this case, light) shining through the paint. Most of the techniques used to achieve this primarily involve the application of paint and then its partial removal with various types of brushes or cloths or even with the fingers, or by scratching away partially dried paint with a variety of implements. The basic techniques are categorized as "tracing" (creating bold opaque outlines) and "matting" (creating the supporting contours and shading).

After painting comes the firing. This is a complex process. Different colours of glass require firing at different temperatures. Different colours of paint or different amounts of paint can all require different kiln temperatures and/or firing times. Real mastery of the subject of firing glass is hard-won.

A unique compound used in stained glass is silverstain. After its special properties were rediscovered at the beginning of the 14th century, within a few years it was being used by stained glass craftsmen throughout Europe — revealing that even in those days information could spread quickly. Silverstain is a silver compound, usually silver nitrate, which when fired reacts with the body of the glass creating a transparent yellow colour. It is this effect of *transparent* bonding that makes silverstain unique. Depending on the glass, the amount of paint used and the temperature and length of firing, a whole range of colours can be produced, ranging from a light lemony yellow to deep amber. Silverstain is often used with coloured glass to brighten reds or to turn blues to green; various shades of silverstain can be mixed with shades of etched flashed glass creating wide ranges of colour in just one piece of glass.

In addition to silverstain, a wide range of enamel colours can be employed. These often require firing at varying temperatures. They result in colours that are relatively "dead" when compared to colour that is inherent in the glass.

Lusters are being used more and more by stained glass artists, particularly by those who tend to opt for float glass

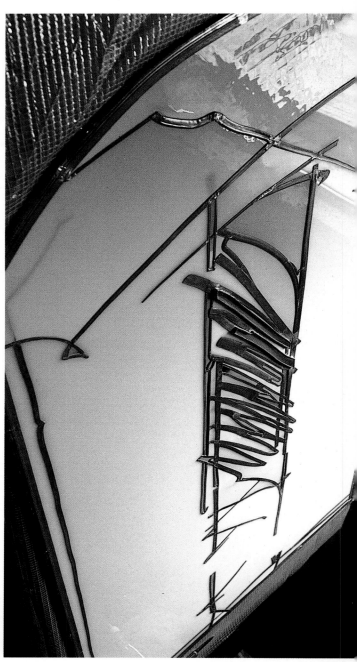

Below *A craftswoman at the Derix Studio, Taunusstein, W. Germany, holds up a piece of etched flash glass to assess the gradation of tone achieved. Acid-etching is a slow process, requiring great care. Sandblasting gives quicker but more limited results.*

Above *Beautiful gradations of tone can be achieved with acid-etching. Some areas of the glass shown here have been masked using a painted resist; while other, more sharply defined areas have been masked with a knife-cut stencil.*

as their medium. The advantage of these paints is their metallic iridescence, as well as the constant temperature needed for firing all the colours — which of course means that several colours can be fired at one time.

Etching

The term "etching" is sometimes used to refer to either sandblasting or acid-etching. Perhaps the most crucial difference between these two is that sandblasting is essentially a simpler and much less time-consuming method, whereas acid-etching is more delicate and capable of much greater subtlety.

Left *This oblique view of a panel by Johannes Schreiter reveals how very tactile and sculpted lead-came can appear. In a face-on photograph it is hard to capture this quality.*

Right *A craftsman prepares the leadwork for a window after the glass has been cut and painted. Stained glass is a labour-intensive activity, and leading panels with many small pieces of glass can be very time-consuming. Skilful and precise cutting of the glass and of the lead makes a window stronger and much neater in the final result. However, it is more often in the quality of the subsequent soldering that one can most clearly observe the quality, or lack of it, in the workmanship.*

Above *After soldering comes cementing — forcing putty into the cracks between the glass and the lead. This process leaves the panel watertight and surprisingly strong.*

In sandblasting, the "mask" or stencil is normally cut out from a paper or plastic material that has been attached by adhesive to the glass. In acid-etching, on the other hand, brushstrokes are more frequently used to paint on the resist: subtle, painterly effects are revealed when the resist is removed.

A problem found with sandblasted glass is its reluctance to release any dirt or grease that it picks up. This makes it particularly ineffective if a window requires to be installed with putty, which tends to be absorbed into the thousands of little crevices in the surface of the glass and cling there with maddening tenacity.

On the other hand, sandblasting is a quick way of cutting through the surface of flash glass. After sandblasting, the glass becomes "opaque" (though still translucent), but this effect can be reversed by a subsequent acid treatment that smooths out the surface. This technique is often called "acid-brightening" or "acid-polishing": not only does it make it possible to clean the glass, but it also adds a sparkle to the matt, non-reflective surface.

Acid-etching is primarily used to modulate the colours of flash glass. If the flashed colour is removed completely, then by working with "white acid" the clear glass left behind can be brought back to a high degree of transparency. Without this secondary etching process, the clear glass is left grey-white and relatively dead, and with little of the original texture of the glass visible.

Lead

Pure lead is the perfect material to serve as a matrix for stained glass. In the early years of this century, various alloys were introduced to lead "came" (characterized by its I-shaped profile) in a spirit of technological development. However, the results of these advances were disastrous. The lead decayed rapidly, becoming brittle and slowly oxidizing virtually into dust.

Other materials are used instead of lead. Zinc, brass and copper, although stiffer and harder to bend into shapes, are quite widely used, particularly in America. These materials work best in designs based on straight lines.

Right *The artist Hans-Günther van Look (on the right) discusses a full-size cartoon with a Derix Studio (Taunusstein) craftsman. Colour selection is always a matter of intensive collaboration. Although the range of colours available is enormous, sometimes glass has to be custom-made to meet an artist's requirements.*

HISTORICAL PERSPECTIVES

Public perception of stained glass as a medium has never truly made the leap from ecclesiastical to secular contexts.

The heyday of secular stained glass was the end of the 19th century, when it was wholeheartedly embraced by most of the famous architects and designers, including Charles Rennie Mackintosh, Adolf Loos, Otto Wagner, Hector Guimard, Antoni Gaudí and Louis Comfort Tiffany.

Most of these figures were part of a mainly ornamental tradition whose impact lasted well into the 20th century. The architect who stands apart from this continuing tradition was Frank Lloyd Wright, whose vision of art and architecture was forward- rather than backward-looking. He saw stained glass as a logical development of the liberation of building design by new materials and methods. With such a potent patron, it is surprising, and tragic, that stained glass failed to become part of the language of modern

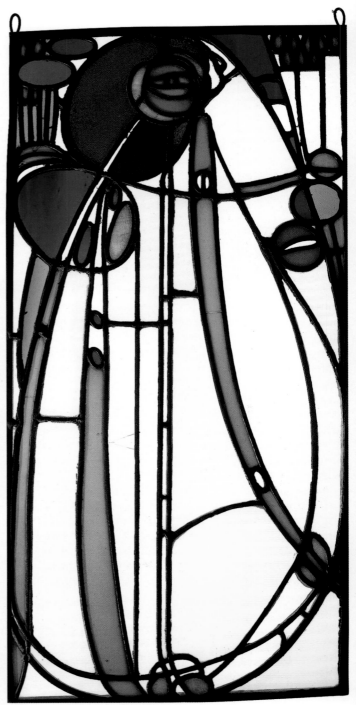

C.R.Mackintosh, glass panel, 1902

John Piper, baptistry window, Coventry Cathedral, England, 1960 (architect: Sir Basil Spence)

architecture. Perhaps this failure is due in some measure to the influence of Mies van der Rohe and Le Corbusier, although the latter actually designed a number of windows and was a great admirer of the medium.

By the 1920s most secular stained glass windows produced, especially in Britain, still reflected the romanticism of the Arts and Crafts Movement and Art Nouveau. The style beautifully expressed by Mackintosh had largely become bastardized into cheap replicas of its

Frank Lloyd Wright, bedroom window, Dana House, Springfield, Illinois, 1903

former glory.

In 1960, John Piper's near-abstract Baptistry window in Coventry Cathedral, England, executed by Patrick Reyntiens, struck many artists and architects as a signal for new things to come. But the religious context made this revolutionary work another cul-de-sac in terms of secular commissions.

The origins of 20th-century glass

Today, stained glass is perceived as an artistic backwater, a craftsman's field, far removed from the central dynamic of artistic evolution. Yet if we look more closely at the key figures in its recent history, we see that stained glass was closely integrated with movements in art, design and architecture in the early 20th century.

Frank Lloyd Wright

Even in the early stained glass of Frank Lloyd Wright we see a language and style that foreshadow, twenty years later, the artistic philosophy of Theo van Doesburg, Piet Mondrian and the whole de Stijl movement.

Most people know that Wright dabbled in stained glass. Many people have seen sample panels of his work and reflected on the purity of design and clarity of thought. But it frequently comes as a surprise when the full extent of his involvement becomes clear. As early as 1889, while still working with the Art Nouveau-influenced Louis Sullivan, he was designing entire walls of stained glass. Almost every building has window after window, wall after wall of leaded glass in his unmistakable idiom. Wright's work was intended as embellishment to his architecture and not as potent

Josef Albers, window, Sommerfeld House, Berlin, 1921 (destroyed) (left)

Josef Albers, detail of Window in Red, 1923

artistic statement, but few artists have demonstrated so clearly the effective use of stained glass as a decorative element, helping to reinforce the motifs of a building.

De Stijl and Theo van Doesberg

The de Stijl movement was started in the Netherlands after the First World War. Collaboration among artists and architects, graphic and industrial designers, and all exponents of the applied arts, was integral to the thinking of the group. The leading participants were Theo van Doesburg and Piet Mondrian. Van Doesburg, the main theoretician and writer, was familiar with Wright's work and greatly admired it; there is little doubt that Wright was a formative influence on the thinking of de Stijl. Van Doesberg was an enthusiast for stained glass and designed many windows himself. By the mid 1920s he had become an influential lecturer, strongly associated with the Bauhaus movement. In 1926, as interior designer, he created stained glass panels for the famous Café L'Aubette in Strasburg (unfortunately destroyed in 1940) — a landmark example of the integration of art and architecture.

The Bauhaus

In Germany in the 1920s stained glass was part of a powerful new architectural movement. When Walter Gropius founded the Bauhaus school of architecture and design (1919-1933), together with Theo van Doesburg and Josef Albers, stained glass was one of the crafts included in the course.

Johann Thorn Prikker, Orange, 1931 (19 x 15in/49 x 39cm)

Many people are surprised to discover that the Bauhaus had a thriving stained glass department. In fact, the smooth and stark language of Bauhaus design was easily translated into stained glass.

Several of the great names associated with the Bauhaus designed stained glass. Paul Klee produced work, as did Josef Albers, whose early apprenticeship in a stained glass workshop inspired a lifelong interest in light, colour and glass. Among other projects (mostly now destroyed or in private collections), Albers designed glass screens for Walter Gropius' Sommerfield House in Berlin (also no longer extant).

Johann Thorn Prikker

A key figure in the creation of a truly "modern" language for stained glass was the Dutch painter and stained glass artist Johann Thorn Prikker. Thorn Prikker was greatly influenced by the de Stijl school as well as by Cubism and the Blaue Reiter thinking of Wassily Kandinsky. After 1920 his stained glass moved away from figurative symbolism and focused on pure abstract language. Unfortunately, few of his later works survive but the 1931 panel *Orange* (left) shows the eloquent minimalist sophistication that he was evolving in his last years.

Heinrich Campendonck and Anton Wendling, both students of Thorn Prikker, continued to search for a new language for stained glass – not always easy in a field still dominated by ecclesiastical commissions.

Post-war Britain

Compared with France, Germany or the United States, relatively little stained glass has been commissioned in Britain since 1945. Only in the last few years has secular stained glass begun to blossom.

John Piper, the distinguished painter, evolved a unique style of stained glass in collaboration with Patrick Reyntiens that was not strictly related to his painting. In many ways John Piper was the last of the great Romantics, using a symbolic language that worked superbly in ecclesiastical contexts but was perhaps too exuberant in its coloration to offer much to secular architecture, particularly the disciplined buildings of this period.

Lawrence Lee, Keith New, Geoffrey Clarke and Anthony Holloway each demonstrated a painterly, florid approach to colour, and a seeming rejection of constructivist ideas — again not entirely in sympathy with the rectilinear architecture of the time. Their work was similar in this respect to that of French artists of the period, but failed to find sufficient outlets to leave an outstanding artistic legacy.

Patrick Reyntiens is not only the executor of John Piper's work, but a superb artist himself. His style has gone through enormous evolution over thirty years, but has always remained centered around the power of the brush, clearly defined form and a bold but finely tuned sense of colour. Like Sowers in America, he has remained a catalyst at the

Anthony Holloway, east window, Manchester Cathedral, England, 1980

heart of British stained glass, encouraging young artists, stimulating aesthetic debate, and helping to bring to Britain the revolutionary ideas from Germany.

In the late 1970s Brian Clarke published his book *Architectural Stained Glass* and demonstrated in his own work that a new language of stained glass was emerging in Britain. Since that time a new breed of artist has now emerged. This younger generation seems to have assimilated the graphic linear language of Germany, so naturally sympathetic to architecture, adding to it the sense of colour and the painterly tradition of English stained glass — will this prove another false beginning or a genuine renaissance?

Contemporary glass in the United States

In America from the 1870s onward, Louis Comfort Tiffany dominated stained glass to such an extent that what we now refer to as an "American opalescent" — a rolled glass developed by Tiffany — was perceived by many people as being synonymous with stained glass generally. Despite some superb architectural works, Tiffany's output is dominated by his lampshades and interior decoration.

As in England, most domestic stained glass until the 1950s was only an extension of the medieval revivalism of the previous century. Although the quality of work by Lawrence Saint and others was excellent, it was essentially outside the mainstream of artistic and architectural evolution.

Since the Second World War there has been no shortage of stained glass commissioned in the United States — both for an active ecclesiastical market and for secular clients. The scale of the industry is itself impressive. The art is practised by professionals, serious amateurs and hobbyists,

Marc Chagall, Staff Memorial to Dag Hammarskjold and Fifteen Who Died with Him, *United Nations Building, New York, 1964 (12 x 15ft/3.6 x 4.6m) (above)*

Robert Sowers, window, Stephen Wise Free Synagogue (detail), New York City, 1975

and the market is better serviced in terms of suppliers, trade journals and exhibitions than in any other country.

Immediately after the Second World War, religious stained glass was greatly dominated by French artists and studios, notably Jean Barillet, Jacques Duval and Gabrielle Loire. This was part of a major initiative by the French Ministry of Beaux Arts, which caused inroads to be made into both the United States and Japan. Much of the work was executed in *dalle de verre*, a technique in which chunks of glass are embedded in epoxy or concrete. Currently this technique is somewhat out of fashion but it will almost certainly be rediscovered as aesthetics turn back towards a more rugged vocabulary than is now favoured.

Of American artists, Robert Sowers is unquestionably the foremost name after 1945. The publication of his first book *The Lost Art* in 1963, followed by his vast project at Kennedy Airport, brought the medium to the American public's attention. His books, largely researched in Europe, exposed American artists for the first time to the

revolutionary new language that was then developing in Germany, in which lead was exploited as the basis of design.

Currently, there is a profusion of artists and studios working in stained glass. A great deal of experimentation, ingenuity and artistic innovation has been part of this boom, not all successful, but vital to creative evolution. Notable among those who are successfully stretching the technical capacities of glass are Ed Carpenter (see pages 72-6), Lutz Haufschild (pages 88-90), Narcissus Quagliata (pages 59, 96, 117), Ray King and Jamie Carpenter.

Post-war France

In France during the 1950s there was an extraordinary flowering of stained glass, sponsored by the Church and the Government. This was largely based on collaboration between painters and stained glass studios. Henri Matisse, Fernand Léger, Georges Braque, Georges Rouault, Jean Bazaine, Alfred Manessier and Marc Chagall all produced designs. Matisse was nearly eighty when he started designing stained glass. Rouault, although in his youth he had been apprenticed to a stained glass craftsman, was also nearly eighty when he started, and Léger and Braque were both nearly seventy. Of these, Chagall's commitment to glass was clearly the most profound: in the twenty years until his death at the age of 99 he did works in many different countries. However, this blossoming of work by older artists who were already legendary in their own lifetime was inevitably short-lived.

Gabrielle Loire (b.1904), Jean Barillet and Alfred Manessier (b.1911) remain the outstanding French stained glass artists of this century. Gabrielle Loire and his son Jacques (b.1932) have executed commissions all over the world, particularly in the United States. Much of the Loires'

Fernand Léger, window in dalle de verre, *Audincourt Church, France, 1950-52*

Jacques Loire, window, main staircase, Chartres Town Hall, France (29½ × 11½ft/9 × 3.5m) (above)

breathtaking and enormous output has been in *dalle de verre*.

The work of the French post-war stained glass artists was primarily based on a painterly approach, evolved mainly around colour. This was in marked contrast to the graphic lead-based language that was evolving simultaneously in Germany.

The German post-war movement

The most influential movement in stained glass in recent times started in Germany in the post-war years. Its origins go further back, but it was the church building boom in West Germany in the aftermath of the war that impelled the medium to catch up with the advances already seen in other visual arts. Perhaps it was also the need to make a clean break with the past that motivated patrons to seek work that was truly contemporary.

When we contemplate the vast amount of work installed in Germany since 1950, it is clear that much has been mediocre. However, this cannot diminish the impact of the many masterpieces of the period which will hopefully provide inspiration for generations to come.

Georg Meistermann (b.1911) pioneered the artistic liberation of stained glass design in the immediate post-war period. In contrast to Thorn Prikker, Meistermann discarded patterns, ornament and geometry, aiming instead for spontaneous, disturbing, expressionistic movement. Meistermann has to be heralded as the first prolific giant of contemporary stained glass. The excitement and possibilities revealed in his work inspired two other important artists — Ludwig Schaffrath and Johannes Schreiter — to take up the challenge of stained glass design.

Ludwig Schaffrath (b.1924) has produced abundant designs during the last thirty years. He has evolved a more structured language than Meistermann, reflecting

Georg Meistermann, window, Church of St Marien, Koln, W. Germany, 1965 (22½ × 6ft/690 × 180cm)

technological forms and the spirit of contemporary design. As with Meistermann, his work seldom employs paint on glass. His primary aim is the expression of movement, using lead as potent graphic lines, in alliance with powerful, contrasting colours. (See pages 22-27)

Johannes Schreiter (b.1930) has been evolving a totally unique language in stained glass for thirty years. His idiom is primarily stationary, involved with a dialogue about the tensions and harmony of contiguous space. His most outstanding contribution to the vocabulary of stained glass has been the liberation of lead from a functional role. Wandering lead lines are the unmistakable hallmark of his style, frequently tapering to restful pregnant endings, creating an interplay of enigmatic spaces. (See pages 28-33)

Wilhelm Buschulte (b.1923) has been one of the most prolific artists of the post-war years, employing a myriad of styles. Some of the greatest windows based on printed patterns have been his – superb decorative work that transcends mere pattern, taking it into the realm of art. Buschulte was profoundly influenced by the works of Meistermann but the spirit of his style is more engaging, more naive, sometimes almost playful. He forgoes subtlety, yet without achieving vulgarity. Florid, swirling organic shapes and vibrant natural colours move across his windows like living entities.

Other stained glass artists who have contributed the finest work over the last thirty years include Otto Dix, Helmut Lander, Ernest Jansen-Winkeln, Maria Katzgrau, Joachim Klos, Hans Luneborg, Jochem Poensgen, Robert Rexhausen, Herb Schiffer, Hubert Spierling, Hans von Stockhausen and Paul Weigmann. Some of these artists are now dead, others are already in their sixties. Stained glass in Germany is still largely dominated by an old guard, and the new generation waiting in the wings has yet to fully reveal itself.

It is possible that a shift in emphasis is about to occur in stained glass, with the mantle of dominance passing from Germany, where it undoubtedly still rests, to the breed of younger artists now beginning to receive acclaim in Britain and the United States.

Wilhelm Buschulte, chapel window, St Katharine's Hospital, Unna, W. Germany, 1968 (11¾ x 3ft/360 x 90cm)

LUDWIG SCHAFFRATH

**Ludwig Schaffrath
Born Alsdorf, near Aachen,
W. Germany, 1924.**
*Studied at the Schulterschule,
1945-6. Assistant to Professor
Wendling, Architecture
Department, Aachen Technical
College, 1946-53. Has worked in
Alsdorf since 1954. Examples of
his work in glass and mosaic can
be found in more than 150
churches, schools, hospitals and
other public institutions in many
different countries.*

Influenced initially by Meistermann (see page 20), Ludwig
Schaffrath in the early 1950s evolved a style of his own that
has become one of the most potent forces in contemporary
glass. His impact can be clearly seen in the work of younger
artists as far afield as Australia and America. More than
anyone else, he has helped to secularize the language of
stained glass.

Schaffrath's work has never been primarily involved with
colour, but has focused instead on energy, structure, line
and movement. Like Meistermann, he has largely eliminated
painting on glass, using lead as his primary graphic tool.
Because his linework has a mechanistic rather than an
organic quality, he succeeds in reflecting contemporary
forms of design and technology.

His seminal cloister windows at Aachen Cathedral (1962-

65) are executed entirely in transparent colourless glass. The weaving graphic images become floating sculptures in glass and lead. Many other works of this period were monochromatic, reminiscent of *grisaille*, although devoid of painting. By the mid-1960s he was incorporating his most characteristic motif of multiple sweeping parallel lines that direct the eye along predetermined channels.

Even as early as 1952, Schaffrath regarded the exterior view of a window as being as important as the interior view. At the time this was an innovative approach, and one that has added to the force of his impact on contemporary glass. Primarily, however, Schaffrath's influence has been due to the originality and power of his language — one that manipulates the viewer's response, leading the eye through the work in dynamic patterns that enforce a willing subjugation.

Omaya railway station, Japan, 1981
This complex, at a major intersection 20 miles north of Tokyo, is more like a shopping center than a station, with commuters and shoppers blending together in a bustling commercial environment. The window is positioned opposite the main entranceway. At night it can be seen from outside — a rippling pattern of white and dark shapes, with the red lines of the interrupted rectangles highlighted. The entire design is a parable about the town Omaya, whose name comes from a word meaning "ice temple." The shade of red used is the sacred colour of the Japanese temple. The panels that appear black in the photograph are in reality reflective and silvery, illustrating the "ice" and indicating that the window is to be taken as a statement about its onlookers. The central pattern of the window is the structured grid of the city. Symbolizing the waterways surrounding the city are flowing white and blue lines, characteristic of Schaffrath's work, and streaming in from either side are the straight lines of railways and roads. Thus, the window comments on the threat to the city from man's expanding infrastructures.

Anne Frank School, Aachen, W. Germany, 1979
The location of this window (12 × 30ft/3.6 × 9.1m) is a room that accommodates a wide range of the school's activities including drama, meetings and wet afternoon entertainments. Entitled Calligraphic Rhythm, *the work illustrates a flow of writing, using one of the simplest shapes of the alphabet — the letter O — to make a narrative. Read from left to right, the rhythm becomes broken and confused, then reasserts itself. The glass shows an exceptional counterpoint of textures —* transparent danziger, *semi-transparent smoky opalescent, and different shades of near-opaque opalescent. Bordering the work at top and bottom is a seedy clear glass, creating a static, restful frame within which the main activity takes place.*

Priest's Seminary, Aachen, W. Germany, 1982 (below)
On entering this small chapel, the visitor is immediately struck by the right-hand side of the window. The eye then moves from right to left, starting with a barely perceptible red opak *that gradually strengthens in colour towards the altar. The subtlety of shading in the red, achieved by careful selection of glass in the studio and meticulously controlled acid treatment, is one of the remarkable features of this work (5½ × 5ft/1.7 × 1.6m). The myriad lenses create an orderly but joyous symbol of individual souls each pursuing the same goal — a coming together with God.*

Public swimming pool, Übach-Palenburg, W. Germany, 1973 (left and right)
This window, situated in the entrance area of a public pool, is straightforward in its symbolism: a big wave, sea and sky all combine in a flowing synchronized energy. Lenses, like bubbles, evenly punctuate the two main intersecting lines of energy, adding rhythm to the flow of movement that traverses the window. The neutral areas of seedy glass are carefully contrived to make a balanced composition and create a sense of foreground and background. Notice how the transparency of the design increases toward the top of the window, revealing trees outside. The window shows how successfully designs in opal *glass can work from the exterior (right): still visually dramatic, but less textured, the window becomes part of the two-dimensional surface of the building.*

JOHANNES SCHREITER

**Johannes Schreiter
Born Bucholz-Erzgebuge,
W. Germany, 1930.**
*Studied in Münster, Mainz and
Berlin, 1949-57. First stained glass
window design, 1959, for the
church of St Johannes, Kitzingen.
Professor at Frankfurt Academy of
Fine Arts, 1962-87. Since 1980,
lecture tours in UK, USA, Canada,
New Zealand and Australia. Works
exhibited in more than 50
museums throughout the world.
Has designed windows for more
than 50 churches and 20 private
houses. Recent works include
Town Hall, Wiesbaden, W.
Germany, 1989.*

One of the great innovators in stained glass, Johannes
Schreiter has never ceased to be controversial and
experimental. His influence can be seen among many
younger artists. However, the style that he has evolved
stems from such an uncompromising, intensely focused
vision that few can hope even to echo the transcendent
purity of his art.

His work divides into distinct phases, starting in 1959
with a period of active, almost busy, compositions that
evolve to a phase of still, quiet statements. In the late 1960s
a more graphic, structured style became evident.

In the mid-70s the wandering, poised lead-line, so much a
Schreiter signature, became even more pronounced. Most
windows of this phase employ red, often as a simple element
alone, sometimes in a dialogue of different shades. In the
late 70s the famous "fractured" phase begins. Windows often
appear like steel grilles that have been prized apart by
mighty hands — barriers broken by light. This period saw
the beginning of the artist's purist abstractions: line becomes
substance, in a spirit that recalls Japanese calligraphy.

To some, Schreiter's minimalism, stemming from a
deliberate economy of thought and action, can appear
somewhat alienating. In fact his work, though devoid of
romanticism or expressionism, is far from cold. Rather, it is
Bach-like in its discipline, demanding of the viewer an
almost meditative stance. The tiniest variation of line or
nuance of colour is pregnant with vision and beauty.

**Church, Langen, W. Germany,
1985 (below)**
*This church window shows the
care with which Schreiter chooses
every colour: for the studio
executing the work, this
perfectionism can be demanding.
The six windows are integrated by
the red frame. The red dots are
formed, in two separate
treatments, by a brown enamel*
*that has been subsequently
silverstained. The specially blown
grey background glass, with its
warm blue tones, gives the red
added brilliance — a resonating
symbolism that defies precise
explanation. The characteristic
U-shaped motif opening into a
column of light evokes the
fundamental optimism of the
Christian message.*

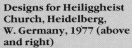

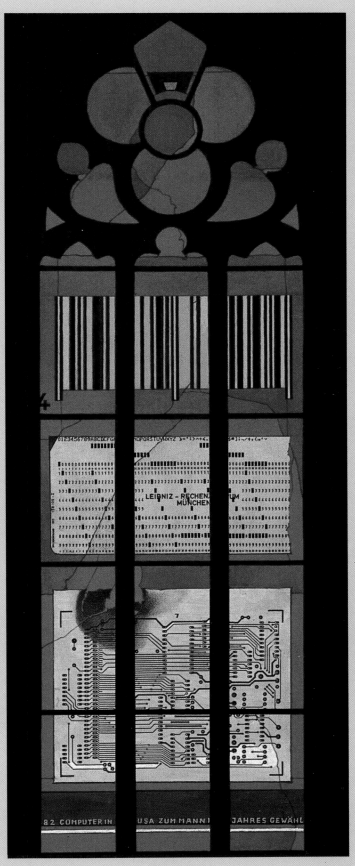

Designs for Heiliggheist Church, Heidelberg, W. Germany, 1977 (above and right)
These two windows are part of a series of twelve designed for the church but, sadly, never installed. However, three have since been commissioned by separate museums. Each window is devoted to an academic subject — a response to the medieval builders' plan to incorporate a library in the side aisles. The two designs here, "Biology" and "Media", demonstrate the iconographic originality of thought that is the hallmark of this artist's contribution to the evolution of stained glass.

Private residence, Hamburg, W. Germany, 1985 (left)
Johannes Schreiter is one of the few artists in stained glass whose work is sought by a select group of collectors. This panel (7½ ft/2.3m high) is in a window opening that was specially cut into the wall of the client's drawing room to accommodate it. The work exhibits Schreiter's characteristic features — vigorous calligraphic line, combined with a sense of finality and completeness.

Frankfurt Airport, W. Germany, 1986 (below)
As often in Schreiter's work, white opaque perspex/plexiglas forms a background for free calligraphic expression combined with precise and highly literal emblems — arrows in opak indicating travel. The very flatness of the perspex emphasizes the texture of the glass and the lead "brushstrokes" which tear across the virgin white surface — a contrast that no photograph can convey. At the top edge, the calligraphic line becomes a framing device, containing the monochrome neutrality of white.

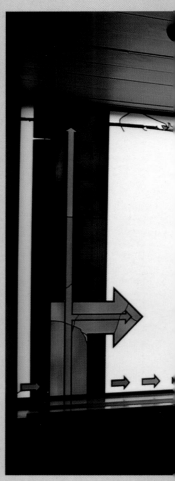

Autonomous panel, 1966 (left)
Originally designed for the wall of a private residence, this panel was executed in 1982 for the Langen Museum in W. Germany. Part of the fascination of the work is the artistic anomaly of having four protruding rectangles of dominant colour suspended above an entirely passive space. The achievement of balance and harmony, with only a jangle of interlocking lines to support the falling weight of the coloured rectangles, is a classic example of the genius of this artist.

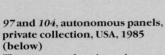

97 and 104, autonomous panels, private collection, USA, 1985 (below)
These two numbered panels are based on the experiences of visiting Bryce Canyon, Utah (97), and the Yellowstone National Park (104). Although the works are abstract in composition, the exquisite colours and subtle modulations of tone are based on "eidetic" images (impressionistic recollections) of these two natural splendours of America.

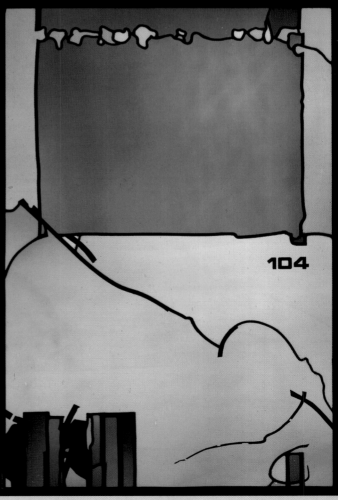

Wedding chamber, Town Hall, Ludwigshafen, W. Germany, 1978 (above)
Within a border of float glass, the white perspex/plexiglas base of this window is accented with a series of angular lines made from lead and glass. Reading from right to left, the lines, based on soft pencil sketches, fade away — terminating on the left side with a row of holes, suggesting a page torn from a ring-bound sketchbook. The lines are neither harsh nor soft, but have elements of both these qualities. They flow, yet with a jagged interrupted force. They are firm and confident, but enigmatic. The work is austere, yet somehow easily approached.

Tribute to Mark Rothko, 1982 (right)
This autonomous panel, now owned by a private collector, is one of a series inspired by Rothko's paintings. Colours lurk behind other colours, and Schreiter's calligraphic devices are subordinated to the central theme of pure abstraction. In defiance of the preconceived limitations of stained glass, Schreiter has responded to the challenge of Rothko's rejection of form.

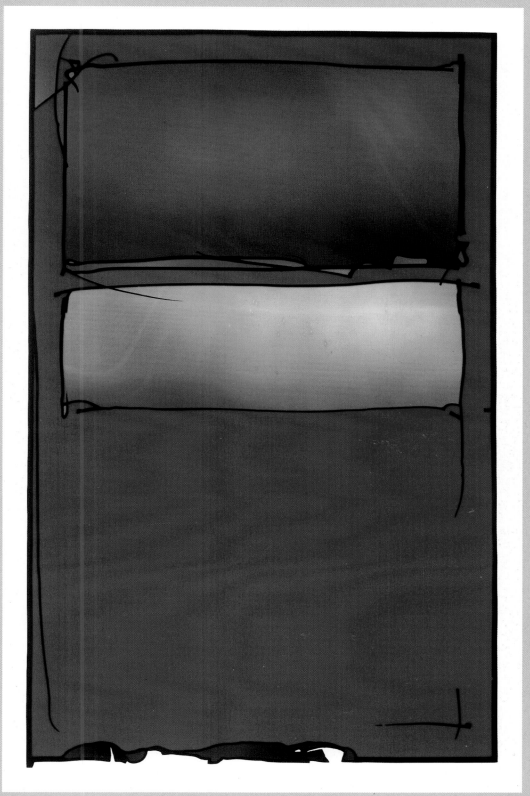

APPROACHES TO DESIGN

Wladimir Olenburg, Fulda, W.Germany, 1988 (left)
This essentially black and white glass screen, 10 feet (3m) square, shows how variations on a pattern can be used to create an effect that is full of interest but by no means strident. The work successfully obscures the courtyard parking lot, and at the same time adds sparkling white light to the office interior. The plain white borders are made in "reflo", an opaque non-reflective glass. Most of the rest of the work is opalescent. However, the areas that show up dark in this photograph are in fact gold, having been gilded and kiln-fired. The arrows in the central square have a metallic finish created by the use of fired platinum on mirrored glass — a technique requiring specialist expertise.

This chapter explores a variety of approaches to designing stained glass windows. Such categorization of design is inevitably artificial; however, it does help to clarify some of the choices that stained glass artists face.

Designing involves making decisions from a range of possibilities that is almost infinite. Commissioning also involves decision-making. Some patrons (or architects) feel daunted by the onus of choice. Commissioning a work of art can be intimidating, and the temptation may be to go for a safe and predictable solution. On the other hand, a piece that is banal quickly becomes boring and superfluous.

Sometimes the budget, even when quite small, can have the effect of forcing an artist to think creatively about how to achieve the desired result. Financial parameters, far from having a dampening effect, can act as a creative stimulus.

Ideally, the criteria imposed on the artist should be general, and based on the role that the client wants the work to fulfil. Often an artist will be able to evolve a concept that achieves the required aims yet differs radically, and greatly for the better, from the client's preconceptions.

Black and white

For many people, stained glass is synonymous with vibrant colour. However, restricting a window to the discipline of black and white (or black and clear) makes the variables of texture and transparency more pronounced. Often the secret of successful stained glass design is to let the glass work for you. The graphic imagery may be restrained, indeed scarcely present, leaving just an interplay of textures to give substance to the work — for example, the cool flatness of opaque white glass, the fluid warmth of clear reamy, the busy intricacy of clear seedy or the mysterious flowing movement of smoky opalescent. The history of this monochromatic approach may be traced back to the painted *grisaille* windows made as early as the 13th century. However, from the 1950s onwards new forms emerged. Ludwig Scaffrath's renowned Aachen Cathedral Cloisters (1962-5) are entirely of colourless transparent glass with writhing lead lines within the traditional Gothic lancets. This monochromatic approach to design has also been extensively explored by Meistermann, Rexhausen, Schreiter and Buschulte, to name but a few.

Ludwig Schaffrath, bank, Aachen, W. Germany, 1986 (this page)
A series of four arched windows (two with doors incorporated) make up the facade of this bank. The windows exploit the differences between clear reamy glass and seedy opalescent. Although the basic grid of thick horizontal bars and arches within arches is identical in each window, the patterns made by the glass and lead show lively variations in their interaction of texture and shape. As well as the clear lenses that are so much a hallmark of Schaffrath's style, coins have been leaded into the windows — visible as dark circles in the photograph (left). The use of leaded glass on the frontage of a bank overturns the usual symbolism. Banks usually have a barricaded, fortress-like appearance; however, this one, thanks to the treatment of the glass (and especially the framing of the doors), has been transformed into something warm and welcoming.

Jochem Poensgen, Police Academy, Münster, W.Germany, 1983 (below and left)
In this window, float glass, mouth-blown opalescent, semi-opalescent and antique danziger *glass are subtly balanced, each complementing the other, the float glass serving as an invisible, interpenetrating frame in which the pattern is suspended. The crispness of the design (see detail, left) is a persuasive rebuttal to those who believe that the hand craftsmanship of leaded glass is alien to the precision of modern building. In this work, every line that we see is lead. Theoretically, the same patterns could have been achieved with paint, or even by printing on glass, but the three-dimensional, tactile quality that is so much a part of the live experience of the work would have been lost.*

Wilhelm Buschulte, public assembly building, Frankfurt, W. Germany, 1986 (below)
This window by a prolific artist is not typical of his often rippling, richly coloured style. However, it is a fine example of stained glasss used to elucidate the architecture. The simple linear design, with its crystal-like rods and subtle textures, is perfectly in harmony with the tall, narrow, arched opening.

Black and white plus colour

Elaborating on a simple, graphic lead-and-glass design by the addition of one colour can have an impact that is quite disproportionate to the actual amount of colour used. Incorporating bold colourful accents that offset the rest of the window helps to fix the image in one's mind. In medieval windows, and during the Art Nouveau period, black and white was often combined with the golden colour of silverstain. Opting for a single colour with black tends to give a work "decorative" rather than "artistic" qualities, so that the design is integrated more successfully into its architectural context. In stained glass, restraint is frequently the key to excellence.

Jochem Poensgen, church, Dundenheim, W. Germany, 1977 (left)
Here, the colour makes a stronger statement than in the crematorium window by the same artist (above), and the underlying pattern is more complex. Bands of cool green flash glass, acid-etched, achieve a balance around the vertical axis.

Jochem Poensgen, Crematorium, Ludvika, Sweden, 1985 (above)
In a background of danziger glass, a simple, dignified, almost heraldic pattern of smoky opalescent strips is punctuated with graduated tones of golden silverstain. The design was partly a response to existing patterns in the crematorium's exterior brickwork.

Float glass

A number of artists are building up a reputation for either mixing float glass with antique glass or working exclusively with float glass. The advantages are the great saving in the cost of raw materials and the greater size in which single panels can be made. Float glass can be successfully painted or airbrushed with black paint, silverstain, enamels or lusters. All these paints require firing to bind to paint to the glass, often requiring a larger kiln than most stained glass artists possess. Surrounding an antique glass design with an area of clear float glass often gives the unexpected impression that the work is suspended in a space of its own, detached from the building in which it occurs. Sandblasted or etched float glass can work superbly with antique glass, either as a centerpiece or as a frame.

Bodo Schramm, exhibition center, Münster, W. Germany, 1987 (left and below)

The two photographs on this page show a large-scale project — around 65 × 10 ft (20 × 3.1m) — in which opak *glass is incorporated as narrow columns of colour within a broad expanse of curved glazed wall. The contrast of the rather dead opacity of* opak *with the pure transparent float glass (blurred by rain in the view below) is highly successful. Schramm revels in the graphic potential of lead, varying the thickness of the leading even within a single straight line.*

Karl Traut, private residence, Taunus, W.Germany, 1987 (above and right)

Each room in this house has stained glass windows of similar design, with a central vertical strip acid-etched from yellow antique glass; however, the different motifs and colours give a unique flavour to each living space. In the window, right, the blue glass has been crossed by sandblasted lines and subsequently treated with acid etching. In the windows above, the float glass is juxtaposed with transparent antique glass, creating a subdued contrast — often more compatible with a domestic setting than the contrast of float and opaque illustrated in the Schramm window, left.

Jane Macdonald, screen, private residence, England, 1986 (above)

This image of a Venetian-style palazzo has been executed on the inside surfaces of two layers of toughened float glass brought together to make a double-glazed screen: thus, it has an intriguing three-dimensional effect. Once installed, assemblies of this kind are easy to clean and their worked surfaces are protected from damage. The designs here have been achieved by a combination of sandblasting, acid-etching and painting with lusters.

Albinas Elskus, panel, 1985 (right)

Made by the New York-based artist at The Pilchuk School, Stanwood, Washington, this 6 ft (180 cm) panel is a single sheet of 8mm float glass painted with black enamel and silverstain. The glass has been acid-etched in the center to create sail-shaped areas of opacity. Although designed as a self-contained display piece, the work has powerful implications for the potential of large-scale painted designs in float glass.

Jürgen Hafner, Justice Center, Regensburg, W. Germany, 1987 (this page)

Seen from the outside (left), this 5-story pentagonal stairwell stands out as the main feature of an otherwise plain building, exploiting the lead to maximum effect. Placing the secondary glazing on the inside of the windows has made the exterior a bold metal relief sculpture, with additional interest supplied by a column of colour. The pattern is subtly different on every story, punctuated by curling irregularities like flourishes in a signature. Marking off the story divisions are bands of danziger glass. At the top of the stairwell (right), the columns of colour rise towards a dramatic canopy. From inside (below) the Mondrian-like pattern of coloured opal glass stands out in vivid relief. Given the cost of mouth-blown glass, float glass used in this way facilitates a budget-conscious solution.

Pattern

The success of a building often depends upon its detailing, which frequently consists of repeated elements on both facade and interior. In the same way, repeated patterns have been fundamental, historically, to architectural stained glass. The most common use of pattern is in the borders of windows, providing a visual frame for the central feature, and thus helping to integrate the work into its setting. Pattern can also be given a more intrinsic role, as an unassertive decoration that catches the eye without upstaging the building. This approach is currently out of favour, yet offers exciting scope to those designers courageous enough to break the boundaries of fashion.

Maritime Hotel, Hanover, W.Germany, 1987 (below and right)
This very simple design, based on a grid pattern, is crisp and distinctive from the outside, reinforcing the inherent patterning of the building (below). From the inside the effect is subdued, softening the room's boundaries while emphasizing its separation from the street beyond. Note the amber-tinted borders, and the cast faceted prisms at the intersections of the grid (shown in the detail, right).

Jochem Poensgen, church of St Georg, Bleibach, E.Germany, 1977 (below)
Each of the large triangular windows here consists of two membranes of machine-made textured glass, with small amber triangles of handblown antique glass. Vertical and diagonal elements in the pattern create an effect of dazzling complexity. The space between the two layers in each window ensures that the design changes as the visitor walks around the church.

Maria McClafferty, rose window, Alexandra Palace, London, 1987 (this page)

The Alexandra Palace, originally built in 1873, suffered the third major fire of its history in 1980 and has recently been restored. The rose window, which features in all three pictures here, is based on the original structure of mullions but the pattern within that structure is entirely new. The window is designed to blend with the restored interior paintwork (below). Despite the vast scale of the Grand Hall (395 × 180 ft/120 × 55m in area; 100ft/31m high), the striking wall decorations, the mirrored glass on the side walls and the floating white "sail" ceiling, it is the stained glass window that claims the eye — not as a contrast but as a focus. The exterior view (left) shows the pattern in more detail. The outer band consists of interlocking blue and white triangles; the inner band contains diamond shapes with yellow and brown glass in an alternating pattern. The white pieces in the window are all mirrored cladding glass, and from the outside in daylight appear as bright reflective surfaces. In the dawn sunlight they make a shining, welcoming star.

All the windows here employ the technique of printing on glass — a cost-effective way to reproduce a pattern. Usually, this is done in either black enamel or silverstain. The paint is silkscreened onto the glass and fired in the normal way. This approach can be combined with hand painting. Some artists print a wax resist onto flash glass and then acid-etch to create either different shades of colour, or areas of colour combined with clear glass.

Brian Clarke, Mosque, King Khalid International Airport, Ryadh, Saudi Arabia, 1983 (left and below)
Nowhere has abstract pattern been more exploited than in the Islamic world. Especially in the last twenty years, stained glass has been installed in thousands of buildings in the Middle East. The brightness of the sun makes it possible to draw upon a richness of colour that is hard to work with in more temperate climates. The heat of the region makes the cool light cast indoors by deep blues and greens a welcome feature. This 22,000 sq ft (2,000 sq m) airport commission is a classic of complex pattern, using bold colours yet tranquil in its overall effect. The panel shown here (left) has an arched section of complex leading surrounded by a pair of simple borders in green antique glass with a black silkscreened interlaced pattern. Although clearly labour-intensive, and thus costly, the leading of the central section has a superb textural quality. Far from being merely a way to join the glass, the lead is an intrinsic part of the work — a relief pattern, like a carving. It thus presents a contrast with the printed borders, whose flatness is appropriate to their subsidiary role. This juxtaposition can be clearly seen in the detail below.

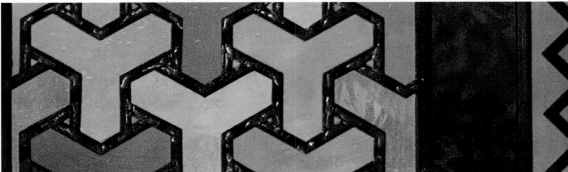

Lutz Haufschild, Burnaby Jamatkhana, Burnaby, British Columbia, 1984 (left, above and above right)
The photographs here show two different areas of the Burnaby mosque. The screen (left) is float glass stencilled with silverstain on both sides and fired at a high temperature to produce the deep amber colour. Silverstain is a transparent medium; hence, the patterns cast a golden light, with tinted shadows. The three-dimensional window shown above (from outside and inside) is one of eight windows in one-inch (25mm thick) cast

opalescent glass printed on both sides in silverstain to create a shimmering moiré effect as the visitor walks past. The artist was inspired by screens at the Taj Mahal and the Alhambra, Spain.

Debora Coombs, model for hospital project, 1984 (below)
This scale model of a projected hospital design shows how simple motifs can be repeated to build up an active pattern that is at the same time relaxing. This design has never been made; however, it would be possible to approach its execution either using lead joints or by silkscreening.

Rectilinear

The roots of a rectilinear approach to design reach back before the Second World War. Since 1945 the leading protagonist of this approach has been Joachim Klos. Although his celebrated contemporaries Schreiter, Schaffrath and, even earlier, the celebrated Meistermann have all exploited rectilinear patterns successfully, Klos has gone further, often building a frame of parallel horizontals as a base for background imagery, which may be either figurative or architectural in content.

Such an approach has a built-in sympathy with the architectural context of which the glass becomes a part. In Klos's work the rhythm created by the apparently endless repetition of a graphic motif is simply a background for a visual "melody." It is the interaction between the cool, mechanistic pattern and the bold, brilliantly coloured detail that gives the work its power.

The designs of artists such as Frank Lloyd Wright and Thorn Prikker, and movements such as de Stijl, the Bauhaus and Art Deco, have been largely based on a rectilinear approach.

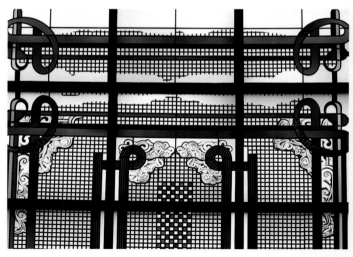

Jochim Klos, church, Katernberg, W. Germany, 1986-7 (this page)
The project shown in the three pictures on this page, more than 5000 sq ft/480 sq m in area, employs both printed glass and leaded glass, all of it opak. (In the detail, right, the flat printed grid and the three-dimensional, curvilinear leading can easily be distinguished.) A work on this scale depends on its own carefully thought-out economics. By using a large proportion of silkscreened glass, costs have been brought

down, leaving the artist free to make a more individual contribution in specially selected areas. The simple printed grid is brought to life in places by primary colour "cornices" (right), with black paint splashed on like spilled ink. The centerpiece (below) is a pink sunburst, contained within a bold gridwork that is left deliberately ragged along the top, as with the uneven grid in the panel above, right. The composition as a whole has a structured primitivism that bursts into song at key points.

Joachim Klos, private residence, W. Germany, 1986 (above)
In this small panel (around 24 in/0.6m square) blue flash glass, worked with acid to create a high transparency, has been used as the basis for a horizontal checkerboard pattern broken in the center — like a seawall breached by storms. The diagonal lines have been used to create a central "knot" of energy, but without disturbing the equilibrium of the whole. The flower motifs occupying some of the squares have been applied in black paint.

Joachim Klos, Rainbow Window, Walbeck Church, W. Germany, 1975 (right)
This is a classic example of Klos's work — very bold and simple. Horizontal leading, closely spaced, forms a rectilinear rhythm within the grid of the Gothic stone tracery. Against this geometric background two elements stand out in vivid contrast — the almost tenderly rendered architectural drawing and the boldly coloured cross. In the right-hand section these two elements intersect, the cross overlapping a classical pediment, from which it leaps forward in a blaze of energy.

David Pearl, The Grand Theatre, Swansea, Wales, 1987 (this page)
For the theater renovation shown in these three views, the locally based artist produced an uncomplicated design, using a simple geometric pattern and fields of interacting colour in unpainted opal glass, contrived to highlight the building at night. An inviting aura is created, welcoming the visitor. On the main facade (right) the design simply follows the curve of the arch. On the restaurant wall (below; interior, left) the effect is rather more complex: the central window presents a grid within a grid, echoed by the small upper windows at either side of the plain oriel. The choice of different shades of blue in this pair of upper windows adds interest to a design that is otherwise symmetrical.

Figurative

The tradition of figurative representation on glass is currently in decline, yet offers enormous potential to those who can free themselves of the pervasive predilection for the abstract. In theory, any figure in a work of fine art can be accurately rendered in glass using the basic repertoire of techniques — etched flashed glass, silverstain, black paint and coloured enamels. Traditionally, the figure is simplified into flat areas of colour and outlined by dense black leading, in the medieval manner. Some contemporary artists, however, take a different approach, treating the glass exactly like a blank canvas or piece of drawing paper. Although painting and firing on glass is time-consuming and expensive, there are, theoretically, few limitations to the sensitivity of tonal variations and fine shading that can be achieved with acid and brushwork on glass.

Traditional design, Japanese lady, private house, 1976 (left)
This exquisite portrait is entirely made in opal *glass, with paint depicting the face and skilful acid etching creating the white pattern on the red cloth. The lady floats in a background of clear* danziger *glass that has been leaded into a simple grid. Each piece in this background has been numbered after cutting and leaded to retain the original flowing pattern of the glass. Although parts of this window would have been extremely costly and time-consuming to make, a large proportion of it is very simple in design, ensuring that the total cost could be kept within bounds.*

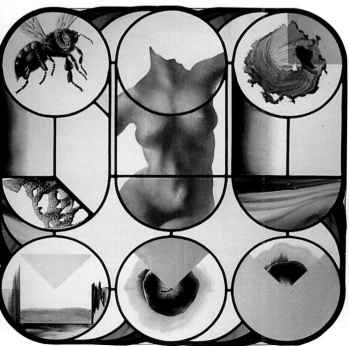

Albinas Elskus, *Eve and the Apple*, small exhibition panel, 1986 (left)
This panel (26 x 26in/66 x 66cm) by one of the world's masters of figurative painting shows the beautiful shaded tones that can be achieved in paint and silverstain. It is a work that overturns traditional preconceptions. The superbly realistic torso and wasp are balanced by looser mineral motifs, and by flat areas of yellow created by silverstain.

John Clark, parrot (detail of restaurant ceiling), Glasgow, Scotland, 1987 (above)
Richness of detail and simplicity of outline are combined in the work of this Glaswegian artist. The brilliantly realistic parrot featured here is made of red and blue flash glass. Seven distinct stages were involved — two phases of etching, two of painting (black and yellow silverstain), two firings, and finally the leading.

Rosalind Grimshaw, *Sleeping Baby*, private residence, Bristol, England, 1984 (left)
Craftsmanship of a high order is a hallmark of this artist's figurative brushwork. This panel of a child, depicted in a naturalistic sleeping position, with every fold of skin and drapery minutely rendered, is a small gem of glass painting, worked in black and silverstain.

Murdoch Associates, ceiling panel, Calendar's Restaurant, Reading, England, 1987 (above)
Intended as a "conversation piece," this simply executed backlit ceiling panel shows that there is a place for humour in stained glass.

The diameter of the piece is 98 in (2.5m). Around the inner circle twelve space cartoon images are etched on blue flash glass. Detail is provided by black enamel and by silverstain fired at different temperatures so that the colour varies from yellow to a deepish red. Around the outer circle are painted Roman numerals, a steam train, and waiters and waitresses in slapstick cartoon postures.

Albinas Elskus, *Arilda*, panel, 1983 (above)
A light opal antique glass is the background for this exhibition panel, 24 in (6 cm) in diameter.

Silverstain and black enamel have been used for the central portrait and the stylized flowers. The control in the "matting" (to create shading) is superb.

Rosalind Grimshaw, *Two Children*, private residence, Bath, England, 1986 (right)
This artist specializes in child portraits: compare the example here with the more subdued treatment on page 49. The "fabric" *of the sofa is red flash glass etched and silverstained, and the skin tones are achieved by "matted" silverstain and black toning. A family portrait of this kind makes a wonderful domestic commission.*

"Glass canvas"

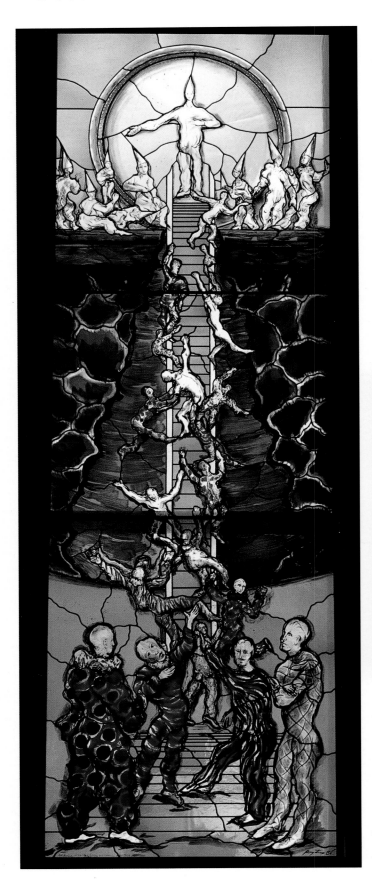

Only very exceptional stained glass artists have the dedication or means to evolve or pursue a personal quest, similar to that of the painter. This is partly because the potential for stained glass treated simply as backlit panels has not yet been realized.

The artist who creates a "glass canvas" makes no concession to space or context, any more than a painter does when he or she starts something new. The work is sufficient unto itself — an autonomous panel. This approach to design is different from anything considered in this book so far. Unquestionably, the leading exponent is Johannes Schreiter, who was a painter long before he became acquainted with glass. His critics still maintain that his architectural work shows a lack of concession to its surroundings, but this is debatable. (See also pages 28-33)

All the panels shown here are notable for their richness of texture, achieved by detailed working into the glass, adding with paint, subtracting with acid. Some artists in this field like their work to be seen only by natural light, which gives a three-dimensional quality — a kind of secret richness. Others design their work specifically for controlled artificial light, immune from the vagaries of daylight.

Patrick Reyntiens, *Fool's Paradise*, 1986 (left)
Reyntiens is not only one of the great catalysts of stained glass over the last 20 years, but is also a unique artist in his own right. Few artists work into the material so extensively and with such consummate ease. This autonomous panel (120 x 40in/3 x 1m) is a kind of inverted Last Judgment based on Jacob's Ladder, with clowns at the bottom and fools at the top — an enigmatic work full of symbolic allusions.

Klaus Zimmer, panel for World Glass Now Exhibition, Sapporo, Japan, 1988 (above)
At the center of this panel (27 x 27in/70 x 70cm) is a cypher, roughly brushed yet poised and still, like a Japanese character. The "frame," built up with glass sections and moulded lead and solder, resembles bronze cast from a finger-sculpted mould. Zimmer continually stretches the capabilities of the medium, combining the painterly with the sculptural.

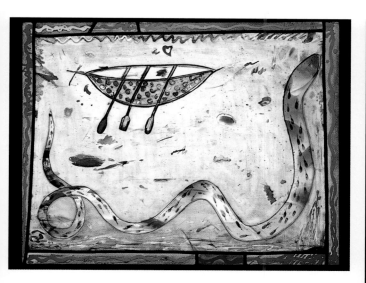

Ursula Huth, panel, 1988
Although capable of working within the context of a specific interior, Huth's natural instinct is to work on autonomous "canvases." Colour is the essence of her work. With cryptic images placed seemingly at random, she creates a language that is poised between the figurative and abstract — richly suggestive but always elusive in meaning.

Klaus Zimmer, *The Aboriginals*, New Parliament House, Canberra, Australia, 1988
This panel (36 × 43 ft/11 × 13m) draws on the art and culture of the Aborigines. Structurally, each panel is like an oriental carpet, but the colours are richer and more decorative — reflecting the Pacific culture in which Australia has a share. As in the other Zimmer panel here (opposite, right), we see the sculpted lead work — almost reminiscent of the work of Narcissus Quagliata.

Hans-G. van Look, Santa Cecilia, Cadaqués, Spain, 1983 (right)
This panel, 13 feet (4m) tall, creates a wonderful sense of space and depth. Although the work is essentially figurative, van Look's graphic interruptions create a series of planes, as if different perspectives are at play. The saint is enclosed in a kind of trompe l'œil *architectural frame. The result is intriguing, forcing the eye to move over the panel, which in turn makes the turned figure strangely elusive, as if in a private dimension of her own.*

DOMESTIC GLASS

Klaus Gemündt, sliding door, private residence, W. Germany, 1986

A large sliding door presents an opportunity for a design that changes radically as the moving panel is opened or closed. Here the artist has aimed at a high degree of transparency, bringing the landscape beyond into the window. At the same time, the opal and danziger glass, and the two blocks of yellow, create a greater sense of intimacy and enclosure than plain glass would have achieved. The two panels are approximate reversals of each other — the upper half of one echoing the lower half of the other, and vice versa. Notice also the shadow effect around the blocks of yellow, giving them a three-dimensional appearance.

Most homes have at least one window that would benefit from the magic of stained glass. The opportunities are particularly rich in doors, stairwells, bathrooms, kitchens, internal screens and conservatories. Some works are designed to obscure the outside view, wholly or partially, while some create a kind of dialogue between interior and exterior — for example, the use of plant motifs would be an obvious allusion to a garden glimpsed through the design. Stained glass used ornamentally as a door surround can create a degree of privacy, yet at the same time have a warm, welcoming ambience. Domestic stained glass has its own design criteria. Many people like a traditional feel; indeed, the following pages do include variations on traditional themes. However, the best work is individual, requiring an imaginative leap on the past of the artist.

Klaus Gemündt, private residence, 1983 (right)
Combining danziger *and opalescent glass with clear lenses, this window simulates a garden pergola. The concentric arches introduce a softer note to the basic rectangular structure.*

Klaus Gemündt, conservatory, 1984 (below)
Danziger *glass provides the background for a* trompe l'œil *of a tree and balustraded wall. The work creates a pleasing bridge between interior and exterior. The mullions of thin steel holding the glass around the door take up little space visually, so that the door seems to be self-supporting.*

Klaus Gemündt, private residence, 1983 (above)
Suitable for a door or corridor, this window of classic design shows a variety of texture and transparency within a small area. There are four different ingredients: a background of clear danziger *glass, clear seedy glass borders and central panel, horizontal bevelled rods, and American opalescent (Tiffany) glass providing colour at top and bottom.*

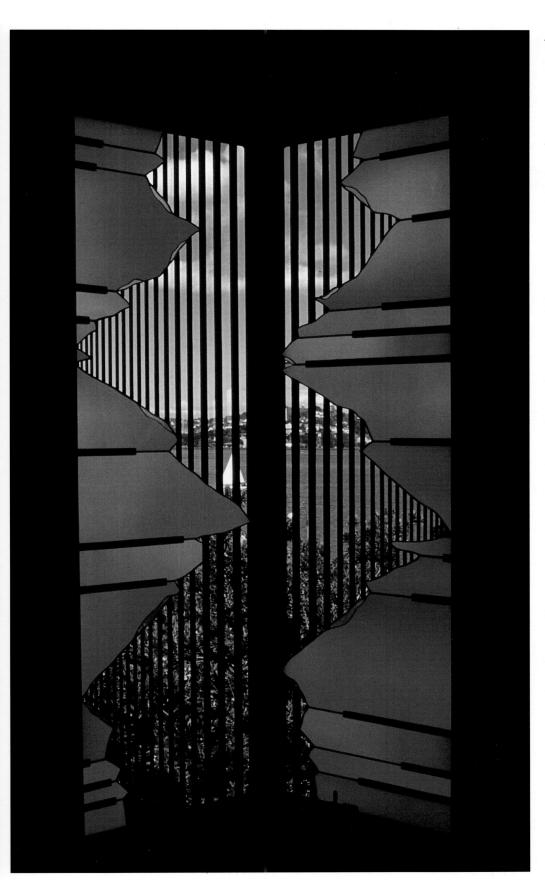

James Walker, private residence, Sydney Harbour, 1984
An oriel window that partly obscures a view of Sydney Harbour adds an element of intrigue, without compromising the beauty of the setting. The warm tone of the intense blue opak *glass is enhanced by the small punctuation marks of deep pink. The fractured edges set up a dynamic tension with the structured verticals that articulate the float glass.*

Hans-Günther van Look, private house near Wiesbaden, W. Germany, 1984 (left)
By the usual standards of van Look's work, this is a simple window. It illustrates the use of opaque glass to enclose a modern staircase, obscuring the view and bringing a deep warm light into the stairwell. The trio of windows is framed within a simple freehand diamond pattern on a background of graduated blue. The deep red opal glass, separated from the grid by strips of plain white glass, has a natural glow, caused by the shifting intensity of colour within each piece. The design is broken at the top (and less conspicuously at the bottom), creating a dramatic effect like that of a vandalized wire fence. The white glass at the top throws ample light onto the landing area at the top of the stairs.

Narcissus Quagliata, penthouse, New York City, 1988 (below and right)
This screen divides a Park Avenue penthouse apartment from a balcony, which offers fine views over the city. The work includes a mixture of antique and opal glass. Clear bevelled strips and brilliantly restrained coloured lines create a beautiful rainbow-like halo. The roundel in the top right corner (detail, right) is characteristic of Quagliata's work: it was specially executed for this project by the famous Venetian glass blower, Lino Tagliapietra.

David Pearl, Great Missenden Abbey, Buckinghamshire, England, 1988 (all three pictures)

By day, beautiful shafts of coloured light pour from the new stained glass windows into the south-facing rooms of the recently renovated abbey (below and right). By night (left) splashes of joyful colour animate the facade. Confronted with the task of producing a contemporary design for these windows of clean-lined tracery, David Pearl opted for a simple watercolour approach. The designs are spontaneous and unstructured, yet look perfectly at home in their setting, without any sense of contrivance. The panels are almost all of etched flash glass — excellent examples of how this medium can be used to create a purely abstract painterly effect.

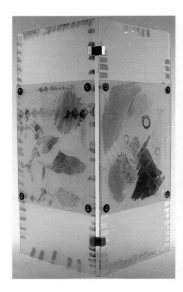

Jane Macdonald, folding screen, private residence, Gloucestershire, England, 1986 (above)

Colourful fish images animate the two smaller panels of this functional opaque screen, which has been sandblasted, acid-etched and painted, and then mounted onto a pair of hinged 6mm (¹⁄₄in) float glass sheets. These sheets have themselves been sandblasted and lightly painted around the edges. In the right-hand panel some areas have been left transparent, allowing secondary images and colours to shine through from behind.

Jane Macdonald, door panels, private residence, Gloucestershire, England, 1985 (right)

These panels are each made up of two sheets of glass, sealed to make a double-glazed unit. The inside surface of each panel has been sandblasted, acid-etched, bevelled (brilliant-cut), painted with lusters and fired. Lusters are distinct from the enamels more commonly used in stained glass, in that they are more transparent and show an iridescence within the colour. The panels, whose imagery is based on two well-known gardens in Somerset, in the south of England, are excellent examples of the painterly watercolour effects that characterize this artist's work.

Annie Ross-Davis, private residence, London, 1985 (below)

This pair of Post-Modern door panels shows a great sense of form, with a contrast of flat and relief design. The bottom triangle, with its beautifully sculpted drapery painted on white opalescent glass, forces the eye upward through a narrative of squares, circles and prisms to the dome motif at the apex, where the drapery is repeated.

David J.C. Wilson, private residence, Florida, 1984 (right and below right)

An impressive lobby area such as this (right) calls for a stylish treatment in the glass. The door and two matching windows at either side have a simple pattern that blends well with the intricacy of the tiled floor. The details beneath the main picture (below right) show two views of the door from inside.

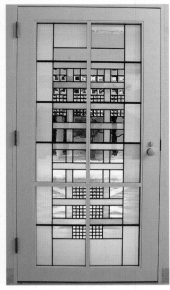

These two details (above and above right) are from the central door in David J. C. Wilson's project in Florida (see the broader view, top, and accompanying caption). In the left-hand detail, notice how two lines of curved leading have *been introduced to break the symmetry. The effectiveness of the door comes partly from the pyramids and bevelled cubes of glass (right), which create a shimmering effect as the viewer changes position.*

Klaus Gemündt, bathroom, Munich, W.Germany, 1987 (above)
A semi-circular bathroom window provides an opportunity for gentle humour in the stained glass — a trompe l'œil *towel balanced on the opposite side by a cluster of fake pipes. The rich blue adds colour to the beautifully stark décor.*

Margarethe Keith, double doors, Quackenbrück, W. Germany, 1987
Elegant understatement is the keynote of these doors (seen in their broader context in the picture, right) that lead from a landing to a main bedroom. White prisms, bordered in a light transparent opalescent glass, geometrically emphasize the Post-Modernist form of the doors. In direct sunlight these pyramid-shaped glass embellishments throw rainbow tints onto the walls opposite; and when the doors are opened or closed an iridescent sparkle bounces off the moving facets of glass. This effect is typical of Margarethe Keith's work — formal and precise, yet with a note of cheerful brightness.

Margarethe Keith, bedroom, Oestrich, W.Germany, 1988 (right)

This is another example of Margaret Keith's witty approach to domestic trompe l'œil. *In the crystal ball held by the outstretched hand, we see the world outside. The drapery, pleasingly asymmetrical, is effectively rendered in different shades of opalescent glass.*

Margarethe Keith, skylight, Quackenbrück, W.Germany, 1988 (below)

A pitched skylight often presents an excellent opportunity for a suspended ceiling in stained glass. This example is unusually transparent, bringing a rich warm light into the stairwell. A poetic touch is the suggestion of canvas sheets with leaves and débris strewn as if wind-blown onto the roof.

Margarethe Keith, dining room, Oestrich, W.Germany, 1988 (below)

In the same house as the bedroom window (left), the dining room presents a further variation on the theme of illusory drapery. The double-take effect is carefully staged. First, we realize that the curtain is part of the window, and then we probably detect that the venetian blind is made of ribbed glass; but it usually takes a few seconds before we grasp that the studded chair is also a playful deception in glass.

Ryoichi Mitsuya, hall of private residence, Japan, 1983 (left)
There is a Japanese saying that roughly translates, "A good entrance invites good luck into a home." This hallway window is designed to provide just such a welcoming atmosphere. The client is an art collector, with many paintings on view in his house. To reflect this interest, Mitsuya has introduced a wide range of pastel colours in an overlapping pattern of screens. The window provides an enticing frame to the exterior view, which is visible in the central upper area of clear danziger glass. *The two side grids are clear antique glass, sandblasted except for two streaks of transparency that move diagonally out from the hub of the window.*

E. Mandelbaum, Amherst, Massachusetts, 1986 (left and right)
This window is an abstract representation of Spring in a series showing the Four Seasons. The arched top softens the simple rectangular frame, enhancing the lovely view outside. The side windows are plain. The design is rich in detail, incorporating suggestive images in black paint and silverstain, with acid-etching. The detail (left) shows the unusual style of brushwork and the subtle acid-etched band in the smoky opalescent, which continues the leaded diagonal from the adjacent part of the design.

Ryoichi Mitsuya, apartment building, 1986 (left)
Three panels of float glass at the bottom of this stairwell window reveal a garden beyond, but the work itself is opaque, blocking the exterior view — except for a single pane of opalescent glass which has been etched to create irregular transparent apertures. The central motif, in shades that harmonize with the brickwork, dramatically bisects the zigzagging silhouette of the staircase.

Ryoichi Mitsuya, convalescent home, Japan, 1983 (below)
This hospital window (5 × 6½ ft/1.5 × 2m), adjacent to a staircase, has a hidden symbolism: blue dots with whiplash tails represent souls transmigrating from one life to another. At a more mundane level the artist "wished to make going up and down stairs more enjoyable through visual movement." The glass is opaque, except for two small "windows" of transparency.

Kazumi Ikemoto, lodge, Nagano, Japan, 1985 (left)
This is a simple window within a window. Deep opaque colours form an outer frame, inside which clear antique glass is set into a simple square "leaded light" pattern. Rippling across the whole window are transparent blue and green reflections in a beautiful mélange of tones, subtly embroidered with tiny etched red and yellow punctuation marks.

Patrick Ross-Smith, private residence, Edinburgh, Scotland, 1985 (right)
The Scottish artist Ross-Smith based these austerely rectilinear designs around electronic music symbols, as befitted his client's profession. The lower blue panel, acid-etched from blue opal glass, *is balanced by a leaded green panel above. This is a convincing demonstration of stark modernist design, not often seen in a domestic setting.*

Claire Waymouth, conservatory, London, 1988 (above and left)
A design of leaves and bunches of grapes, with detailing painted in black, has obvious aptness for this conservatory with Gothic windows. From inside (left) the view to the garden is filtered through contrasts of opalescent and clear glass. The side windows contain a central panel of smoky opalescent glass with a clear border so that they hint at, rather than reveal, the view of the garden beyond.

Amber Hiscott, hallway, Scotland, 1983 (below)
Based on a single sheet of float glass, this hallway window has been achieved by a mixture of sandblasting, acid-etching, brilliant-cutting, and bonding of small pieces of coloured antique glass. The flowing design creates a pleasing interaction between the plane of the glass and the natural forms outside. The added coloured glass creates warmth, as well as giving a structure to the basically organic imagery.

Keith Gale, kitchen, Bristol, England, 1987 (above and left)
Although rich in detail and activity, with plant-like forms against a yellow and turquoise grid, this window is nevertheless relaxed in mood. It brings into the room bright and fresh colours which contrast with the reddish tones of the decor. The central panel at the top of the window, with its vigorous yellow "scribble," provides a focus for the eye. The two-tone border (detail, left) has been achieved by "plating" a yellow antique glass behind an acid-etched green flash glass.

Karl Traut, private residence, Wiesbaden, W. Germany, 1986 (right)
Purposely designed to restrict the view from both outside and inside, this minimalist window successfully resolves the problem of an asymmetrical window frame. The focus of the window is created by "plating" two pieces of etched flash glass, one blue, the other red. The resultant interweaving of colour, poised on the short side of the frame, creates a perfectly balanced composition: nothing could be added or subtracted without doing damage to the whole.

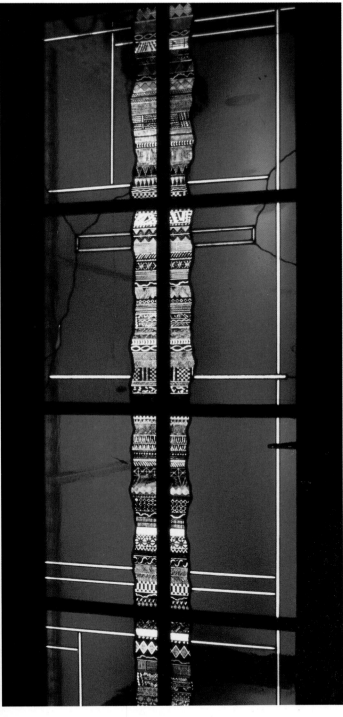

Herman Blondeel, door, Ghent, Belgium, 1986 (above)
Eight small panels make up this door between a kitchen and a corridor. The band of plain blue reveals down the center, as if parted, a succession of intricately worked designs loosely derived from Arab and African patterns. This central column is made up of different grisailles, silverstain and enamels. Touches of red and yellow and an asymmetrical grid of white glass create additional interest. Perhaps the blue could have borne being even plainer, leaving attention rivetted on the detailed brushwork, so often a feature of Blondeel's work: nevertheless the contrasts of colour, content and scale make this a richly rewarding piece.

ED CARPENTER

Ed Carpenter
Born Los Angeles, 1946.
Studied stained glass design and technique with Patrick Reyntiens in Buckinghamshire, England, 1973. With a grant from the Graham Foundation for Advanced Study in the Fine Arts, became apprenticed to Ludwig Schaffrath in Alsdorf, W. Germany, 1975. Currently runs his practice from Portland, Oregon. His designs are fabricated by Tim O'Neill. Other projects include: skylight for Aberdeen Office Tower, Dallas, Texas, 1986; First Community Church, Dallas, Texas, 1987.

In a memorable phrase, Ed Carpenter once said that he tries to make his windows look as if they are "hatched from the same egg as the building." He is especially fascinated by the process of working with architects to evolve suitable sites for stained glass — "where the building pauses to ask for detail." He is most at home with buildings that are based on a hierarchy of large- and small-scale elements rather than on relentless repetition of identical motifs. The glass must harmonize not only with the structure of the building but also with its function — circulation routes can be boldly treated, but work spaces and gathering places demand more restraint. Colours outside are often allowed to make their own contribution: because these natural hues change with the cycle of daylight, a transparent window is potentially more interesting, in Carpenter's opinion, than the more static effect of brightly coloured glass. Characteristically, there is a sense of light and airiness in Carpenter's work. Classical poise is the prevalent mood.

Kaiser Permanente Medical Center, Portland, Oregon, 1985 (all three pictures)
Ed Carpenter's conviction that the role of stained glass is not so much to create an image as to transform the view by modulating light is eloquently illustrated by his entrance window for the Portland Kaiser Clinic, shown in all three pictures here. The work measures 24 x 14 ft (7.3 x 4.25m). Understated in its colouring, it is designed to convey an appropriate mood of gravity and calm. The diagonal lattice pattern is extrapolated from the radial arrangement of architectural members in the gable. Prismatic pyramids set symmetrically into the window provide attractive punctuation.

Justice Center, Portland, Oregon, 1983

Ed Carpenter's 30 ft (9m) arched window for the west lobby of the Portland Justice Center (shown in all three pictures here) epitomizes his concern that glass design should serve, and take its tone from, the architecture. Beautifully symmetrical, the window gives dignified presence to the doorway, and animates the lobby with its interplay of light and shadows. Seen from inside (right), it borrows colour from the trees and architecture beyond. This is a fine example of an essentially "black and white" window whose life is contained in the contrasting textures — white *opal glass, rich* danziger *antique, and cast bevelled pieces, adding sparkle.*

Skylight, Oregon Institute of Technology, Klamath Falls, Oregon, 1988 (this page)
The impact of this skylight, designed in collaboration with S.R.G. Partnership, Portland, depends largely on the way in which it serves as a giant lens, splashing a kaleidoscope of colours over the off-white walls of the interior. Measuring 60 x 32 x 15 ft (18 x 9.75 x 4.6m), the structure includes mirrors, hundreds of crystalline prisms, as well as strips of two types of dichroic glass (below right and below left). Dichroic glass has the property of changing from one colour to another depending on the direction of incoming light or the angle of view: the overall effect is of constant change, according to the time of day, weather and season.

BRIAN CLARKE

Undoubtedly one of the most important stained glass artists in the world today, Brian Clarke is exceptional in reconciling a strong personal vision with an ability to integrate his work into the language of the architecture.

Although primarily a painter, Clarke perceived early on in his career how stained glass offered the possibility of working on a "canvas" of truly giant scale. The most recognizable feature of his style has been a palette restricted to just the four primary colours, used to create a deceptively simple language that has extraordinary eloquence. Typically, his work features a lattice or grid to which amorphous interruptions of colour (which he calls "amorphs") add subversive life. A frequent motif is the cross, imbued with almost magic potency by its graphic simplicity and by centuries of accumulated symbolism.

Brian Clarke
Born Oldham, Lancashire, England, 1953.
In 1978 was a consultant with John Piper to Festival of the City of London GLASS/LIGHT exhibition. Has recently worked in Japan; exhibited at the Seibu Museum of Art, Tokyo. Major retrospective, Hessisches Landesmuseum, Darmstadt, 1988-9. Currently based in Kensington, London. Other major projects include: Queen's Medical Centre, Nottingham, 1977-8; Olympus Optical Building, Hamburg, 1981; Mosque at King Khalid Airport, Ryadh, Saudi Arabia, 1983 (see page 45); Golf Club, Lake Saga-mi, Japan, 1989.

Conference room, Endell Street, London, 1981 (this page)
This window shows Clarke's capacity for restraint. A blue background divided into a simple grid creates implicit calm. The smoky opalescent panels of the inserted red-bordered "windows" are broken by wriggling tendrils of glass and light, defying the imposed structure. The work shows a typical Clarke theme — a tension of order and chaos.

"The Chelsea Window," backlit panel, London, 1986-7 (right)
Designed concurrently with the Buxton project (see pages 82-3), this work shows an obvious similarity of motif, but the design is less of a narrative, more a pure expression of beauty in all its profusion. Although the panel as shown here appears opaque (as is often the case with backlit panels), it is in fact made entirely of transparent antique glass; and when it is backlit, as intended, with uplighters and downlighters, the eye floats through the blues and greens but is arrested by the more opaque reds and yellows, which burn into the retina. The piece is a microcosm expressing some of the basic contrasts of life — the seasons, fire and ice, engagement and isolation.

Olympus Optical GmbH, Hamburg, W. Germany, 1981 (above and right)
"Let the glass work for you" is the maxim that underlies these minimalist office windows. Basic fields of colour are edged with contrasting borders. In the white and red windows, the grid-like design is broken by unobtrusive "squiggles"; the blue and green windows are more regular (right). Although designed more as "canvases" than as integral parts of the building, these windows justify their location by filling the office space with an ever-changing and unique experience of light and colour. From outside at night the windows are experienced on a totally different scale — as a bold band of colour across the frontage.

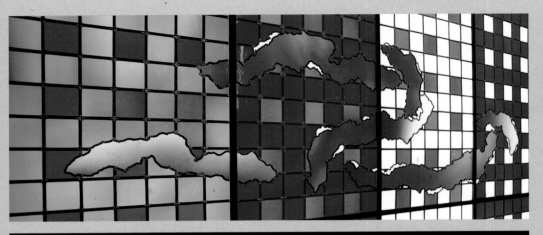

Spectral Screen, 1988 (this page)
In this panel, 13 feet (4m) square, we see an evolution of Brian Clarke's style from the curving, smooth-edged organic motifs of Buxton (pages 82-3) and the Chelsea Window (page 79) to the use of more disruptive amorphic elements. Unlike most artists, Clarke designs stained glass as a collage, assembling a series of handpainted pieces of paper. This is analogous to the execution of stained glass: hence, the design and execution form a continuum of language that gives an inherent integrity to the artist's work. In this panel the basic grid structure, made up of a sequence of interlocked colours, is disturbed by the agitated silhouettes that threaten and dislocate the static purity of the background.

The Proscenium, Leeds, England, 1990 (right)
This illustration shows part of the original design for a 9,470 square-foot (880 sq m) project — a covered shopping mall, based around a beautiful Victorian street. The figures in the foreground give a sense of the overall scale. A 260-feet-long (80m) roof ridge and two 82-feet-long (25m) entrance canopies provide an exceptional role for controlled but dramatic use of stained glass. Again, we see in Brian Clarke's design his mastery of the medium — an exact balance of the predictable and the unpredictable. First, he creates a continuous framework — in this case, blue. Contained within this secure context is a dynamic interplay of colour fields, dramatically in motion. Finally, cutting across this rich but orderly background are just a few powerful, living elements. It is a work on a massive scale — unprecedented in secular stained glass in the UK.

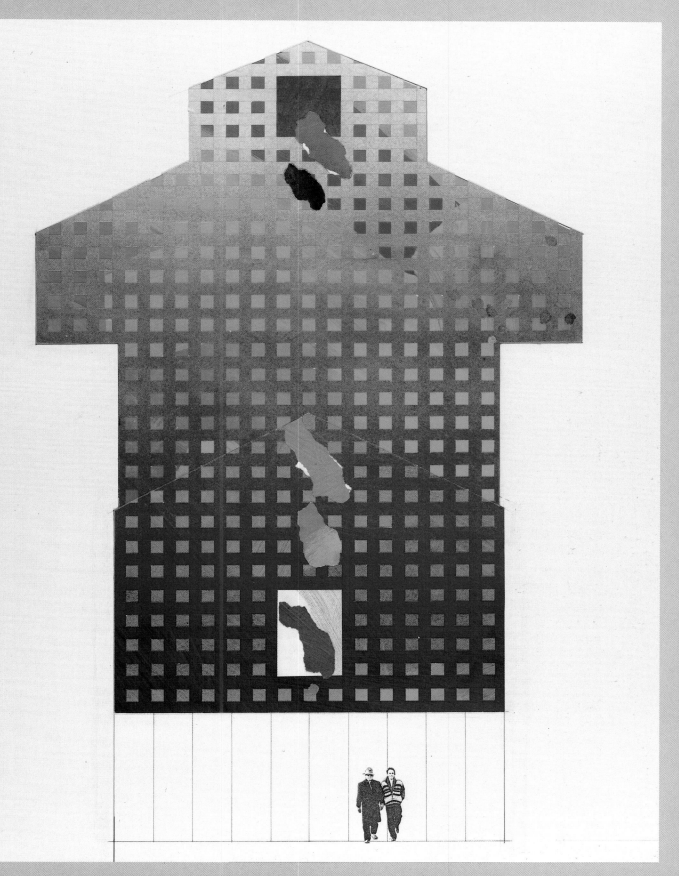

Shopping mall, Buxton, Derbyshire, England, 1987

When the Derbyshire Historic Buildings Trust decided to convert the old thermal baths building into a shopping mall, Brian Clarke was asked to design a 3,000 sq ft (280 sq m) barrel vault over the central atrium area. The five pictures here show different views of the project. The stained glass vault is suspended from a steel purlin structure and entirely sealed with an external polycarbonate shell. Contained within a reticent frame of pure green glass are twin seas of transparent blue (left), forming a background for regiments of organic motifs in greens and blues, golds and yellows, full of anarchic potency (detail, above center). At the apex, where the vault explodes in a blaze of white, the shapes break free of their boundaries, embracing each other in a celebration of life.

The bold primary colours of the work project a joyous vitality that communicates to the widest possible audience. At a deeper level, there is a clear, richly symbolic dialogue between the mechanistic and the organic.

Having lunch in the arcade's restaurant, we see the glass soaring up with vivid proximity only a few feet from our chair. But to be fully appreciated, the work has also to be seen in its wider perspective. Driving down from the hills at night, we come upon this radiant jewel of light shining up from the valley — a beacon, irresistibly beckoning.

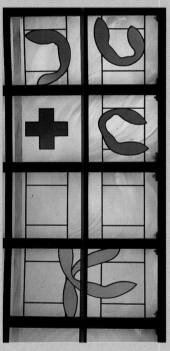

PUBLIC BUILDINGS

Most public buildings have areas that are experienced only in transit — lobbies, stairwells, atriums. This sort of space can so easily become orthodox and anonymous. However, there is a potential here for strong, bold statements in glass, not simply as appended artefacts, but as statements that are integral with the fabric and the experience of the building.

The current trend for building large complexes under glass, such as shopping malls, provides opportunities for works on a large scale. Stained glass can also transform spaces that are in continuous occupation, such as offices: here the intention is often to humanize a mass-produced environment.

Susan Bradbury, Newcastle-upon-Tyne School of Art and Design, England, 1987 (right and below)
Sponsored by the City of Newcastle, this 270 sq ft (25 sq m) art college project creates a stimulating but peaceful environment in a room that is used sometimes for work, sometimes as a reception area for visitors. The window is essentially simple, based on flowing line and

subtle variations of tone. A restrained blue and grey palette was deemed suitable, as the room itself would often house a colourful cacophany of art students' work. Because colours in the work are kept to a minimum, texture is emphasized by the use of danziger glass. As so often, the window has benefitted from having borders. Together with the glazing bars, these hold together the graceful, weaving movements of form and line that constitute the melody of the piece — the sandblasted line, like a coastline on a map, and the garland-like shapes, which create a carnival feeling. The borders are orchestrated so that the darker shades are at the bottom: this creates a rhythm which leads the eye up and down, drawing us into the dance.

A fundamental principle of public stained glass is the need to reconcile the daylight interior view with the exterior view at night, exploiting the full potential of both, bearing in mind the physical characteristics of the building and the image that the client wants to convey.

Stained glass is a kinetic art form. It uses light to work complex transformations, which constantly shift with time and the seasons. At night the building, as it were, turns inside out, the stained glass making a powerful visual statement to visitors and to passers-by. Often, this statement will have symbolic overtones relating to the building's function — for example, a glass design of classical symmetry might evoke a sense of tradition, respectability and poise. Some of the most exciting projects, though, are those in which the expected associations are subverted. Banks might seem to demand a symbolism of impregnability; while cool impartiality might be deemed apt for a justice building. However, both these contexts might benefit from a less predictable approach —

perhaps attempting a warmer, more welcoming mood.

Architects and designers tend to work within a repertoire of solutions to recurrent spatial and design problems — a set of mental approaches as fixed as the items in a tool kit. Sadly, stained glass has a low status in this list of standard responses. By focusing on some notable exceptions to this rule, the following pages celebrate a more enlightened view.

Holly Sanford, District Court Building, Auckland, New Zealand, 1987 (this page)

The trio of entrances to this courthouse, each with a similar overhanging canopy, together comprises 1,615 sq ft (150 sq m) of stained glass. The canopies have a membrane-like quality, that is particularly apparent when looking from the inside (below). The clearly thought-out brief for the artist specified certain qualities to be aimed at — dignity and purpose, stability and calm, humanity, hope and approachability. In addition, "The work must represent those values our society would consider stable throughout time; the work should represent the multicultural makeup of Aukland, and a bi-cultural (Maori) viewpoint." The triangular motifs not only reflect stability and order as the brief required (the triangle is the most stable geometric figure) but also allude to specific Maori taaniko patterns, used in woven cloaks. The structured relationships of the triangles hint at the hierarchy of the judicial system. The warm colours suggest hope and humanity, adding brilliance to an austere building, especially at night (right) when panels that appear grey in the daytime emerge as warm peachy tints.

Holly Sanford, City Council Building, Hamilton, New Zealand, 1985 (this page)
This 581 sq foot (54 sq m) main stairwell window in opak and clear float glass again shows how these two materials can be used in contrast to enhance the sense of space. The blue shapes, like crystals on a microscope slide, appear suspended, as if captured in a jumbled, unstable confusion — a kind of abstract narrative which the visitor explores while ascending the staircase. The most dynamic part of the work is visible immediately upon entering the foyer. The central white column helps to bind the work together, and at the same time leads the eye to a second design upstairs. Mingled among the blue shapes are a few touches of rusty red — punctuation marks that arrest the eye and give depth to the surrounding blue.

Lutz Haufschild, Scotia Place office building, Edmonton, Alberta, 1982 (left and far left)
Entitled the Scotia Diagonal, *this giant piece for an office atrium (1,000 sq ft/92 sq m) is made entirely of unpainted leaded glass, each piece carefully handpicked to produce the movement of colour that is essential to the life of the work. All the glass is opaque, thus obscuring an unattractive outlook. The glass casts constantly changing and rippling swathes of red and gold sunbeams onto the cantilevered wall of windows on the opposite side of the atrium. The detail (left) shows how shaded colour adds interest to a complex grid within a grid. From the outside the building has an assertive look, affirming the strength and confidence of its inhabitants, yet remaining magnetically appealing.*

Lutz Haufschild, Robson Court, Vancouver, British Columbia, 1986 (this page and left)

Courtly Evanescence *is the title of this expressionist window designed for the tall, narrow atrium of a speculative office block (see the general view, right). Measuring 30 x 25 ft (9 x 7.6 m), the window is intended as a focal point opposite the main entrance — a glass mural. Its broad, horizontal, flowing brush strokes (above), sweeping across the back wall as if daubed by some giant hand, make the atrium seem wider and more spacious than it really is. The glass is mostly light opalescent antique glass, airbrushed and painted with blue enamel and silverstain. The L shapes on the blue panels (clearly visible in the detail, far right) are silkscreened black enamel. The cast prisms (also apparent in the detail) are silverstained to add warmth to the overall effect. The plain opalescent grid that encloses the work integrates it smoothly into the structure of the building.*

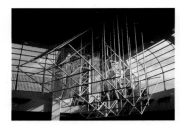

Lutz Haufschild, Sunridge Mall, Calgary, Alberta, 1981 (this page)

The Sunridge Sculpture *is a steel and glass construct, 32 ft (9.75 m) deep in its longest dimension, suspended in a central position from the roof over the mall (top). The work revolves on its vertical axis, moving through one rotation every 45 minutes and presenting to shoppers a changing spectacle of colour and shape. In direct sunlight, the colours are projected onto the interior of the mall (above), imperceptibly moving, but appearing different every time you look.*

Robert Middlestead, States Services Commission Building, Wellington, New Zealand, 1985 (left)
These 20 ft (6 m) panels — part of a series of four — are made in leaded antique glass and hung on steel cables from the ceiling. The design was inspired by Maori weaving patterns.

Richard Spaulding, Volunteer Park Conservatory, Seattle, USA, 1981 (below)
This entrance canopy for a conservatory built in 1912 is a successful blend of modern and traditional. The exact shade of green for the project was specially blown by the Lambert glass factory in Waldsassen, W.Germany. The center of the canopy is decorated with etched lilies, convolvulus and passion-flower. The etched border designs are taken from a range of historic precedents. Eight of the 35 panels were "slumped" (curved in the kiln) to match the curve of the roof.

Linda Lichtman, Millers River Apartments, Cambridge, Massachusetts, 1988 (below)
The title of this work, Glass Columns with Pink, *emphasizes its use of architectural motifs in a framework of float glass. These motifs are combined with natural imagery, worked in paint, so that the work mediates between the manmade world and the world of nature. A collage of grisaille techniques, the window incorporates rustic forms that may be read as leaves, pebbles, seeds or raindrops. A similar ambiguity is seen in the "capitals" of the columns, which may be taken as flames or as sheaves of corn. It is the casual, sketchbook style that gives the piece its richness.*

Linda Lichtman, Lyndon B. Johnson apartments for the elderly, Cambridge, Massachusetts, 1987 (right)
Installed in the lobby of the apartments, this window, entitled Columns and Lintels, *has been carefully thought out in relation to its setting. The atmosphere of the work suggests a celebration of life and nature. Each piece of coloured flash glass has been etched to reveal a suggestive organic shape, and then acid-polished to bring transparency to the clear surrounding glass. Each area of colour has itself been worked into with acid to produce the painterly modulations of tone that are the source of the work's vitality. Finally, black enamel has been applied and a busy and detailed array of primitive imagery has been scratched into the surface (see details, top).*

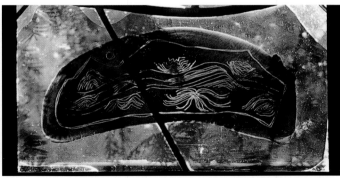

Ursula Huth, door panels, OPD Building, Stuttgart, W. Germany, 1988 (right and far right)
Here are two examples from the 33 door panels designed by Huth for the Stuttgart telecommunications office building. All the panels are based around a theme of communication. Each panel is made of two layers of enamel-painted float glass, enclosing a central sheet of wired glass. The resulting composites form an amazing array of multiple images, each expressed in the mythic language of the child.

Ursula Huth, entrance to school, Leonberg, W. Germany, 1985 (right)
A joyful collage of images in the artist's unique style creates a colourful entrance panel. The snake, the tepees (bottom) and the three-roofed house (top left), symbolic of home, are images that constantly recur in Huth's work. In this panel the "home" image is embraced by a reclining giant. We can enjoy speculating on the symbolism, or just revel in the childlike joie de vivre *these images express.*

Karl-Martin Hartmann, Ahnatal, W. Germany, 1987 (left)
Working within a simple grid structure that echoes the architect's square window frames, these columns of fiery red lead the eye upward to their splattered apex. This artist often makes a feature of relief elements, as seen at the bottom right of this window, where a tall thin panel with antipathetic lateral lines is set in front of the main plane of glazing. One of the main virtues of this design is its sensitive response to the architectural context.

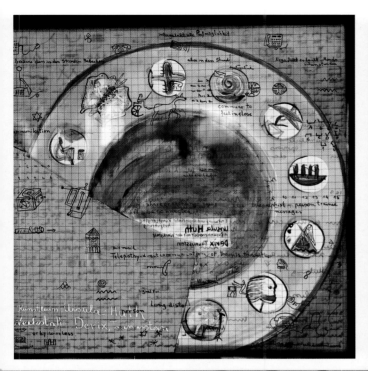

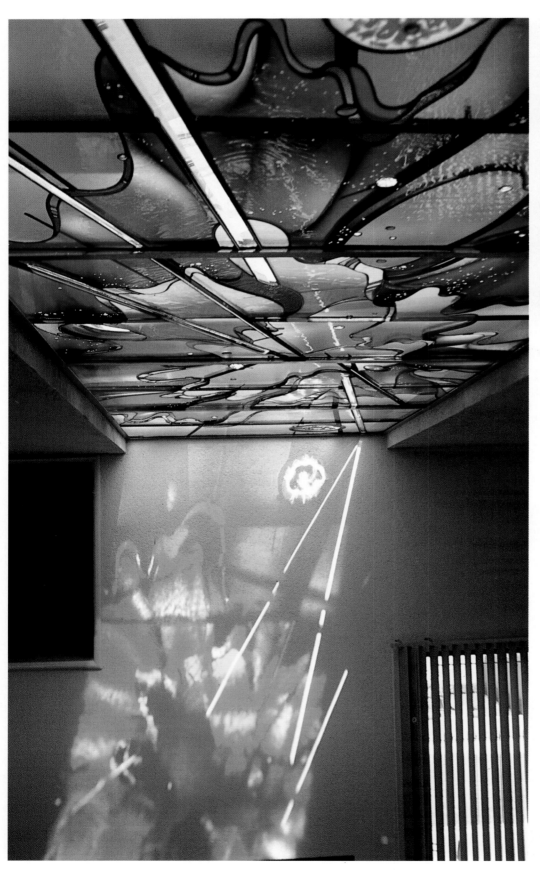

Narcissus Quagliata, *Universe in Red*, reception area, Mexico City, 1989 (left and above)
It is interesting to contrast this florid explosion of colour, culturally compatible with a Mexican environment, with the muted tones of the Park Avenue project (page 59), where colour occupies only tiny fraction of the design. It was partly the very height of the ceiling that enabled Quagliata to risk such richness of tones. The work is entirely made in customized transparent mouth-blown antique glass, mixed with specially created rondels, long linear bevels and two Austrian-made lead crystals.

Richard Spaulding, New York Library (Mid-Manhattan), 1986 (above and right)

Reported to be the first major public commission of stained glass in Manhattan for 50 years, this project took over four years from initial contact with the client to completion. Although, at the outset, there was enthusiasm from all involved, it seemed unclear who was responsible for its funding — a not uncommon experience in stained glass. The red opal glass was specially made by Lambert in W. Germany under the artist's supervision to ensure the exact gradation of colour. Further gradations were created with acid by the artist. Some of the yellow tints were achieved by silverstaining. The design is carefully worked to give warmth to the exterior, making a more welcoming entranceway, and to shed a warm radiant light inside the foyer.

Kenneth von Roenn, J.M.Wright School, Stamford, Connecticut, 1984 (above and left)
This 260 square-foot (24 sq-m) project is situated above the main entrance doors to a school, as shown in the interior view (above). A corridor runs across the lobby at the upper level, directly alongside the window. Running over three sections, the design pivots on a central axis, as expressed by the L-shaped corners. The window is made up of horizontal bevels and transparent mirrored bevels scaled to the dimensions of adjacent brickwork, with red and blue flash glass, white opak and seedy antique glass presenting a wealth of detail. This detail culminates in a complex central flourish (left). Throughout the day, as students come and go, the image of the window traverses the lobby walls and floor. The symmetrical composition reflects the rather static nature of the building, but its waywardly flowing lines suggest a challenge to absolute orthodoxy — individuality sustained.

Kazumi Ikemoto, Tennoji School, Osaka, Japan, 1984 (right)

Mixing etched black opal *with transparent antique glass, this stairwell window creates a hovering, three-dimensional image — a rippling ribbon arrested in spiralling motion. Leading the eye up and down, the design gives a strong, unified character to a neutral space. The blue border in antique glass, pierced with lenses, creates a frame that emphasizes the window's vertical mobility. In contrast are the few diagonal red bands that cut right across the design, in etched gradations of colour.*

Patrick Ross-Smith, Cutlers Gardens, East London, 1986 (left and below left)
When this East India Docks warehouse building in the City of London was recently restored, the Edinburgh-based artist Patrick Ross-Smith was asked to create windows that would work within the constraints of the original steel frames. The resulting rectilinear designs, based on green

and blue colour fields, emphasize
the windows' outlines in a way
that reinforces the conservation
aspect of the project. In the detail
(below left) we see an example of
blue flash glass that has been
acid-etched to achieve beautiful
gradation of colour. Tiny organic
shapes have been left behind,
standing out from the plane of the
surrounding glass as if suspended
in relief.

**Johannes Beeck,
Telecommunications Office,
Flensburg, W. Germany, 1987
(below)**
*Occupying the whole wall in the
cafeteria of a post office
administration building, this
backlit panel shows how much
can be done with a small amount
of colour. Made from* opak *glass,
prisms and silverstained lenses,*

*the mural derives most of its
impact from the intrinsic tonal
life and texture of the white and
grey glass. As in the water of a
flowing river, the window
contains a dialogue of different
vectors of movement, each pulling
in its own direction, but resolved
into harmony by the embracing
green at the bottom and the grid
of prisms above.*

Joachim Klos, Kreisserparkasse Bank, Schwabisch-Gemünd, W.Germany, 1988 (this page)
This ceiling window over the main cashier's hall in a bank, mostly composed of etched flash glass, matches the client's brief with exemplary accuracy. As required, it is a strong design that nevertheless allows the viewer to experience the external architecture. The design is an open one, with some panels of totally clear glass. Although at first sight there seems to be a logic to the patterned design, on closer inspection this turns out to be pleasingly elusive. It is a window that would transform the experience of waiting in line at a cashier's desk from misery to delight.

Karl Traut, Commerz Bank, Hanover, W. Germany, 1988 (left)
Made entirely in opak glass, this backlit ceiling is especially responsive to its architectural setting. The spartan simplicity of its graphic elements, the sweeping curves and in particular the thrusting hemispherical projection, all help to emphasize aspects of the building's design. The focus of muted but expressive colour is held in a simple grid-like frame that reinforces our sense of the interior space. The work is cool, singularly devoid of incidental drama, yet it is precisely this serious, studied quality that makes it suitable for a bank. This type of ceiling is easy to install into a simple T-section suspended grid. Each panel simply slots into place, and is easily removed to replace lights or clean off dust from the glass.

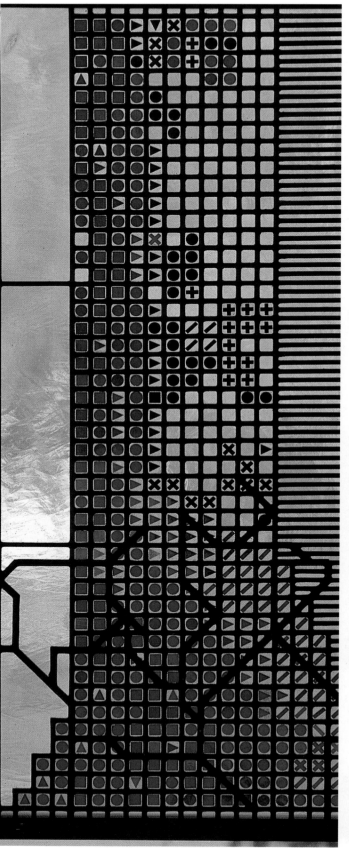

Joachim Klos, Volksbank, Taunusstein, W.Germany, 1985

Few works demand the technical expertise that this contemporary masterpiece by Klos (shown in all three pictures) required of its executors. The work sits alongside a simple single-story spiral staircase in a new bank in a German town. Its achievement is to make the viewer long to mount the stairs, drawn upward by the soaring vertical pattern. Every line we see is lead. Every shape has been etched from blue flash opal glass or stencilled in black. Although the overall mood is cool, the rich texture of the myriad lead lines, the swarming detail of simple geometric shapes, and the sense of movement in the flowing diagonals, all combine to make the work dynamically active and alive. Absolute precision is vital in this kind of piece, so that it bears close inspection (see detail, left): the slightest misalignment or sloppy intersection would extinguish its life. The project is a superb example of the crisp sharpness of line that is possible with leaded glass in the hands of highly skilled craftsmen — a key factor in an age of machine-made building materials.

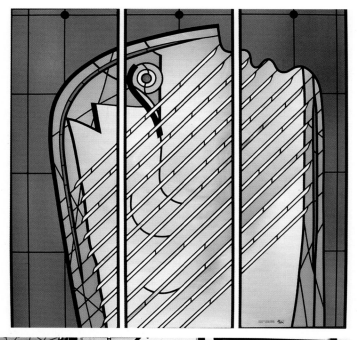

Leifur Breidfjörd, autonomous panel, 1986 (left)
Measuring 70¾ × 70¾in (180 x 180cm), this panel was designed specially for the 1987 "Scandinavian Craft Today" Exhibition at the Seibu Museum, Tokyo. Intended to be backlit, it is made entirely in opal *and* opak *glass.*

Leifur Breidfjörd, International Airport, Keflavik, Iceland, 1987 (right and left)
New airports offer the opportunity for adventurous designs on a large scale. This suspended glass sculpture (right) in dark yellow antique and white opalescent glass (26 × 20 ft/8 × 6 m) is a transparent floating picture hanging parallel to a 45° sloping glass wall in Iceland's new airport, looking out towards the runway. The work captures something of our deepest feelings about the challenge and excitement of flight. At night it is illuminated, and sparkles as reflections from the specially installed lighting system are caught by the separate striations in the antique glass. The detail (left) is from a matching, but paler, window immediately opposite the entranceway of the airport. All three designs by Breidfjörd shown here have a vigorous movement based on staccato graphic linework.

TROMPE L'ŒIL

Restoration of 1905 window, Town hall, Wiesbaden, W. Germany

Architects can add richness, style and even humour to their buildings by quoting from the whole historical vocabulary of architecture. Trompe l'œil *stained glass provides the perfect medium for such allusions, and has the additional effect of helping to integrate a window into its context. The example illustrated here, executed mostly in American opalescent glass, is greatly enlivened by the Corinthian side columns, which bring space and depth to a potentially flat work. The craftsmanship in this window is not of exceptional quality, and the overall effect verges on the vulgar. However, these limitations should not be allowed to obscure the work's considerable virtues: not only the* trompe l'œil *ingredient, but also the fruity border alive with colour, the vivid blue background, and the central eagle, full of strength and* joie de vivre.

Windows that incorporate *trompe l'œil* effects are not widespread: those shown in this section show a potential that is sadly underexploited. Illusions can be used to manipulate our sense of spatial relationships, to blur the distinction between window and building, or to introduce a note of playful virtuosity, or even humour. As with *trompe l'œil* in other media, the primary goal is to create an impression of additional depth — an extra dimension incorporated without using up space. Simulated architectural features can furnish a window with a solid, symmetrical framework, within which other aspects of the design can be more adventurous. Some *trompe l'œil* depends very much on careful painting and shading, but successful results can equally be achieved with simple graphic lines and suitable colour.

John Clark, Princes Square Shopping Centre ceiling, Glasgow, 1987 (below)
A simple backlit suspended ceiling simulates the soaring domed roof of a conservatory, with parrots, plants and snakes against a blue sky, all weaving a rich tapestry of incident and space. Brilliant blues, yellows and reds stand out against the muted background colour. The work reveals a high level of technical competence and figurative accuracy (see page 49). As with most trompe l'œil, *the sense of space is created by lines that follow the rules of perspective, and by the varying shades of colour separating foreground and background.*

Trix Hausmann, The Galleria, Hamburg, W. Germany, 1983 (far right and right)
This wonderful hanging drapery is so vivid when viewed from the inside (far right) that you feel its folds might sway and rustle in a strong breeze. The window is simple, with dark grey and clear antique glass and skilful airbrushing adding to the sense of perspective. The surround of clear float glass allows the design to hang, suspended in space. From the outside (right) the work is equally intriguing, though in a different way: the draped fabric becomes a cascade of metal lines, frozen in a pattern charged with movement.

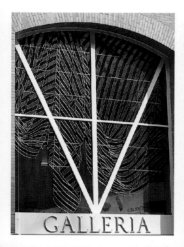

Margarethe Keith, villa, Quakenbrück, W. Germany, 1987 (left)
There is something joyful and extrovert in these welcoming hallway windows. The use of a sharply contrasting colour for the lining helps to clarify the form of the curtains. The blue opal glass has been acid-etched to create shading. Float glass used at the bottom of the windows strengthens our impression that the drapery is hanging in air. The atmosphere of the work is typical of this artist's style (see also pages 64-5).

Klaus Gemündt, private house, Krensel, W. Germany, 1983-8 (above and above left)
Here are two attractive examples of illusionistic glass in a domestic setting. The sense of depth is made more convincing by the vague impression of distant objects beyond the glass. The double doors in the right-hand example here depict a vine-clad garden trellis, whose wooden slats are persuasively shadowed to give them the appearance of solidity. The doors in the left-hand example (above) are more complex. Notice the way in which the grid of tiles in the glass seems to continue the real floor. Here, the picture is like a sign indicating the doors' function: there is a terrace beyond, although of course it looks nothing like the idealized terrace depicted.

Klaus Gemündt, hallway, Paris, 1984 (left)
Smoky opalescent glass forms the background in this mural, while the foreground elements are opaque glass. Much of the work is very simple and inexpensive to make, as only relatively small areas have complex leading. It is striking how lifelike a feeling is created by the different tones of opaque glass used to express the foreground planks.

Hermann Gottfried, cemetery building, Kehl, W.Germany, 1981 (below)
These trompe l'œil *arches are in Gottfried's typical painterly style, but are unusual for him in being so abstract. The simple curtain wall is transformed into something indefinably challenging to our perceptions. The clear suggestion of architectural form is countered by the less substantial sense of a theatre backdrop.*

SCREENS AND BACKLIT PANELS

Screens and backlit panels both offer a way to give life and colour to a public area, such as a boardroom or reception area, or even a domestic interior.

Screens create a division of space that is more psychological than spatial. If they are movable, they allow a flexible arrangement of areas within the overall context of a room. If incorporated into fixed partitioning, a stained glass screen could offer much that is currently supplied in many modern offices by venetian blinds.

Backlit panels offer an opportunity to display stained glass as works of art (see page 52-3). They are especially appropriate in internal spaces where the absence of natural light makes it unlikely that the ambient light of the room will ever be greater than the light source behind the panel.

Basements often present specific design problems that can be successfully resolved using backlit stained glass. Moreover, backlit panels present an option for ceilings where, for whatever reason, a skylight would be inappropriate.

Not infrequently in the course of restoring or modifying a building, window surrounds are ripped out and the windows filled in. This is sad and unnecessary when a backlit stained glass panel could provide a beautiful feature.

Chinks Grylls, screen, 1984 (above)
In contrast with the screen alongside (right), this predominantly red screen by the same artist is mobile in design but static in material. The white opalescent glass contrasts with red opal.

Chinks Grylls, screen for boardroom, London, 1988 (right)
This 6-feet (1.8m) long screen is executed in clear danziger and opal and opak glass, with borders of prisms, and horizontal bands of bevelled glass. The screen is designed to maximize the kinetic effect, changing with every variation in lighting or in the viewer's position. The overall result is a fluid juxtaposition of transparency and translucency.

Jürgen Drewer-Reisinger, *Signs of Life*, 1986 (below)
This young German artist has the rare ability to use primary colours with decisive effect. Here, the subtle gradation of red to orange at the bottom is, executed using red and yellow flash glass. The lead and the painted lines, fluidly used, are almost indistinguishable. With simple designs that have a pure balance of composition and colour, commentary seems almost superfluous.

Jürgen Drewer-Reisinger, *Sunrise*, 1988 (right)
There is always a quality of humour, as well as pathos, in Drewer-Reisinger's work. The rich but simple colours make the work fresh and bright, but the coolness of the bottom panels speaks not so much of night, as of the cold world of humankind from which the sun rises unblemished — or perhaps, despite the title conferred on the work by the artist, the sun is drowning, rendered colourless by the bleakness of our culture.

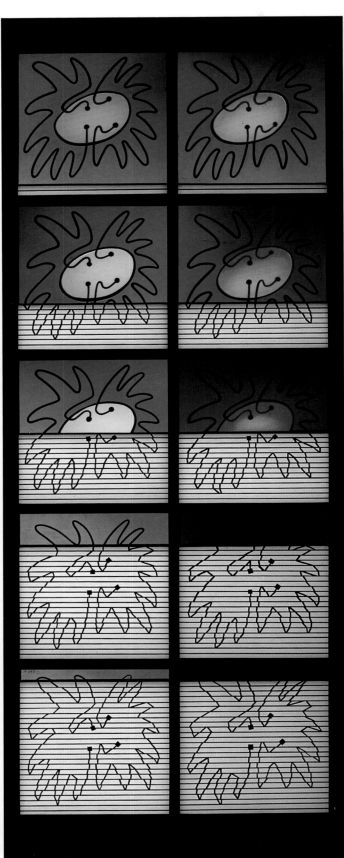

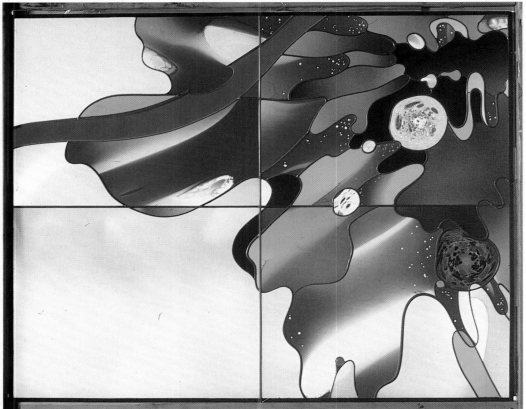

Narcissus Quagliata, office entrance, Oakland, California, 1985 (above)
This backlit panel, entitled Glass Painting *(12 × 50ft/3.7 × 15.2m), is made entirely in transparent antique glass and rondels, which have been specially flashed and blown with gradations of colour to meet the artist's very detailed specifications. Preferring the greater intensity of colour he can achieve with a transparent glass, Quagliata has mounted sandblasted sheets 6 inches (16cm) behind the panel to obscure the fluorescent tubes and the spotlights highlighting particular areas. The lighting system is computerized to match the varying requirements throughout the day and night. This is an exceptional example of a vast "glass canvas." There are no concessions to architecture here, no structural linework — just fluid expressionistic colour.*

Narcissus Quagliata, panel (left)
In this colourful panel, flowing gradations of colour have been blown into flashed glass. Only the clear dots have been achieved by sandblasting.

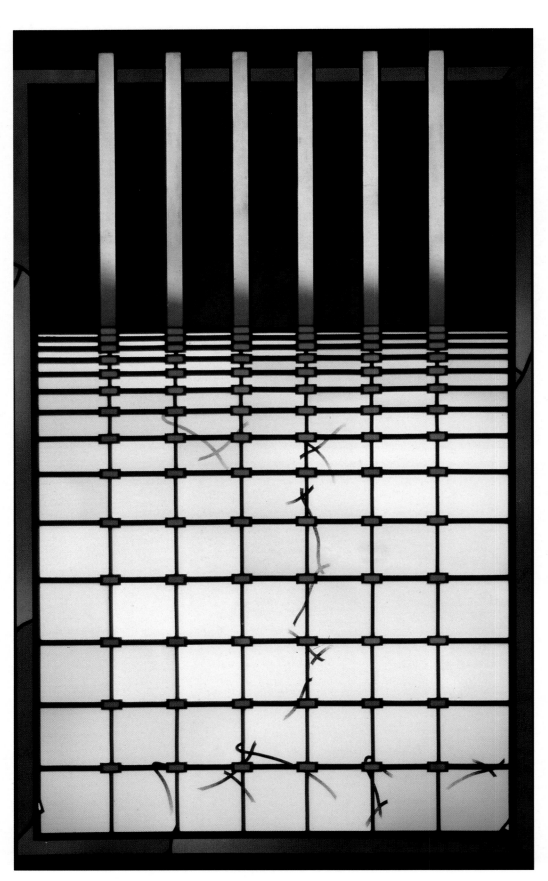

Karl Traut, autonomous panel, 1984 (left)
This highly structured piece is geometric and austere, like much of Karl Traut's work. Looking at the piece in real life, one is struck by the exceptional craftsmanship of the lead and solder work. Colour is used sparingly, which serves only to emphasize the contrast of the blue and red. The red columns at the top of the work are etched flash glass. Despite its restricted vocabulary, the panel succeeds in conjuring up a whole range of images — blood, barbed wire, imprisonment — all expressed behind a mask of graphic purity.

Hermann Gottfried, *Crucifixation*, 1983 (right)
This autonomous panel is arguably one of Gottfried's finest works. His panels are sometimes reminiscent of the painter Modigliani, but in this crucifixation we feel a Germanic influence — a brutality of physical experience, mixed with pathos. The work expresses a quality of emotive force that is not often seen in the vocabulary of figurative stained glass.

Klaus Zimmer, panel, 1985 (far right)
Another example of a "glass canvas" by this Australian artist (compare pages 52-5). Again a frame has been created with moulded lead that gives a focus and intent to the simple abstract image. The "calligraphy" has been reduced to a central blue column, with complementary yellow (silverstained) horizontal brushstrokes — showing the particular skill of this artist to give meaning to the simplest visual expression.

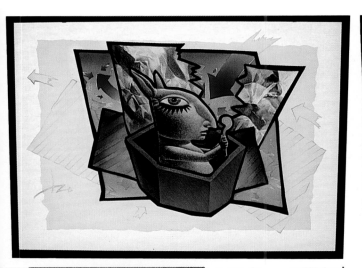

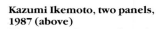

Kazumi Ikemoto, two panels, 1987 (above)
These two works, part of a series of four stylized autonomous panels intended to be mounted on a wall and backlit, show the art of stained glass at its closest contact with mainstream painting. Designed with intricate precision, they show a medieval disregard for perspective and scale. The angular outlines of the central images are softened by a duotone white surround. The luminous quality created by the backlighting seems perfectly appropriate to the surreal, moonlit worlds inhabited by these animistic spirits.

Linda Lichtman, *Snake in the Grass*, 1988 (left)
This autonomous panel, 2 feet (60cm) high, shows two fundamentally different techniques, with correspondingly contrasting results. The dark central section has been worked as if in negative: black paint has been applied to the glass and then scratched away, leaving pencil-thin lines of wonderfully varied colours shining through. On the border, by contrast, acid has etched away almost all the flashed colours, leaving only wavy splashes of colour, sparkling in a clear background, defined and emphasized by parallel black brushstrokes.

Linda Lichtman, *Border Scratchpad*, 1988 (below)
Another autonomous panel, but much more serene. Clearly defined floral shapes stand forward from shaded backgrounds. The border, more regular than in the panel alongside (left), again is made up of etched flashed glass, but here the language of the brush is more varied, more vibrant. Lichtman's work is always restlessly active, in a way that communicates a profound love of nature's endless variety.

Patrick Reyntiens, *Hercules as Harlequin*, 1988 (detail) (left)
Many of Reyntiens' works employ classical, mythic themes as subjects for his interweaving of colour and figuration. This head from a recent autonomous panel shows the spontaneous and varied brushwork. Most of the pieces of glass are painted and fired twice, to achieve different densities of colour. The brushstrokes, executed with legendary rapidity, are mostly left untouched, with only occasional scratching with a quill to achieve controlled highlights.

Patrick Reyntiens, *Competitive Sport*, 1988 (left and above)
This panel shows the incomparable style of one of the most important figures in 20th-century stained glass. Fundamental to Reyntiens' approach is his defiance of the graphic strictures of lead, so that form is not automatically separated by colour and by line. In a post-impressionist synthesis, lead and paint and colour merge into a unified language. The detail (above) shows the audacious use of juxtaposed colours characteristic of Reyntiens' work: in a way unmatched by other artists, his glass resonates with the masterpieces of the Middle Ages, yet clearly springs from the spirit of 20th-century art.

Ingrid Swossiel, bank, Dornbirn, Austria, 1988 (this page)
This 11½-feet (3.5m) square ceiling panel (shown above in the Derix Studios before installation) was made for the cashiers' hall of a bank. Made from sandblasted mirror and various types of opal and opak glass, it is backlit by fluorescent tubes (left). The swirling *dark shapes and cryptic arrows are mirrored glass, in stark contrast with the weaving white opalescent, the painted foliage and the changing colour sequence of the border. This composite of diverse elements makes up a dream-like narrative, as if some mythic saga had been encoded into the work.*

Berin Behn, ceiling panel, Fitzroy House, Adelaide, Australia, 1985 (above)
A series of 15 small skylight panels, totalling 16¹/₂ x 10 feet (5 x 3m), was incorporated into this building when it was refurbished as a corporation headquarters. The panels are made in a mixture of red and blue antique, a rolled wispy opalescent, and a white ribbed glass forming an outer surround. Minor interruptions break into the central opalescent squares and red borders, adding a note of asymmetry.

Karl Traut, private residence, W.Germany, 1984 (right)
Both natural and fluorescent light illuminate this large ceiling panel in a private house. Made in opak and milk glass, the work is 11¹/₂ feet (3.5m) square. Its design is unobtrusive, basically symmetrical, but with uncontrived irregularities. Whiplash swirls of lead soften the impact of the design, and in the central panel are five red dots that relieve the white and cool blues, preventing the panel from appearing rigid.

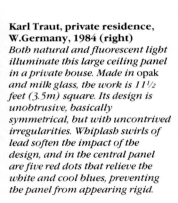

ALEX BELESCHENKO

**Alex Beleschenko
Born Corby, Northamptonshire,
England, 1951**
*Studied painting at Winchester Art
School, 1969-72. Post-graduate
course in printmaking, Slade
School of Fine Art, London, 1975.
Won John Brinkley Fellowship,
1976. Studied architectural
stained glass, Swansea School of
Art, 1978-9. After a spell working
in Sweden, 1980-81, set up stained
glass studio in Exeter 1981. Recent
work includes 45-ft (13m) glass
sculpture in the new Reading
Railway Station Concourse.*

This artist has risen to prominence in Britain very rapidly
over the last few years. The preparation for this emergence
has been a long and thorough training that has given
Beleschenko an exceptionally wide knowledge of the
properties and potential of the medium. Few people have
experimented with such a variety of innovative techniques,
exploiting all the possibilities of etching, brilliant-cutting,
slumping (moulding in the kiln), laminating, lusters
(metallic colours) and traditional leaded glass. Undoubtedly
this artist is pushing back the frontiers of glass.

The outstanding feature of his current work is its
harmonious resonance with contemporary architecture and
design. This is partly due to his successful elimination of
lead. In association with the Derix glass studio (Taunusstein,
W.Germany), he has perfected a technique of pure glass
mosaic (illustrated, right). These "laminated" panels have a
flat, unbroken surface texture that perfectly corresponds to
ordinary glazing and other contemporary cladding materials.

**Hall door panel and fanlight,
1986 (above and right)**
*Enclosed between two sheets of
clear float glass, this essentially
decorative feature is made from
green and purple antique, acid-
etched float glass and brilliant-cut
float glass (see detail, above).
Even with such potentially
frivolous imagery, Beleschenko's*
*constructivist aesthetics create an
authoritative sense of order. A
rising central column of vivid
purple, framed in green and white,
is both interrupted and
emphasized by the graceful
abstract forms of semi-circular
fans. In direct sunlight, the
sparkling fans cast radiant
colours onto the adjacent walls.*

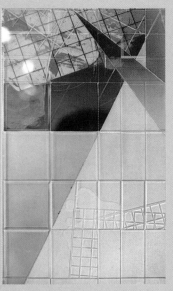

**TWF office, Soho, London, 1988
(this page)**
*This panel in the reception area of
an architects' office is part
partition, part backlit panel. The
work stands immediately behind
the receptionist's desk and matches
the milk glass panels that run the
length of the office (to the right in
the picture, left). Two layers of
worked glass are sandwiched
between clear protective glazing,
making a double mosaic that
incorporates antique and float
glass. Brilliant-cutting,
silverstaining, bevelling and acid
etching (see detail, above) have
all been employed to produce a
panel that is subtle and muted:
the design blends beautifully with
the high-tech minimalist office
interior, yet makes a strong
statement about the creative
sophistication of its sponsors.*

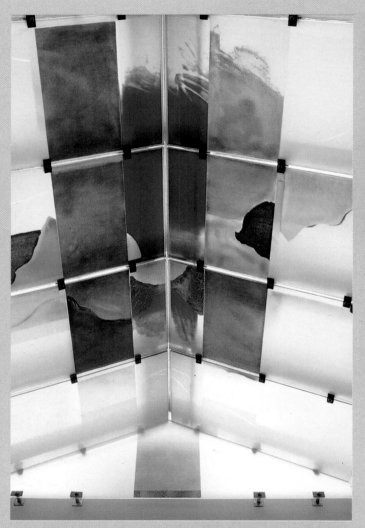

Sutherland's Restaurant, Soho, London, 1987 (above and left)
Suspended on long threaded bolts beneath a glazed skylight, this pitched roof design forms the central feature in a Soho restaurant. Although the technique used is similar to that of Stockley Park, in this case Beleschenko has created the detail of the design not by a mosaic of tiny glass pieces but by etching and painting onto larger pieces of coloured flashed glass. The work has a sophistication that reflects well on its environment, creating a subtle, finely tuned glow.

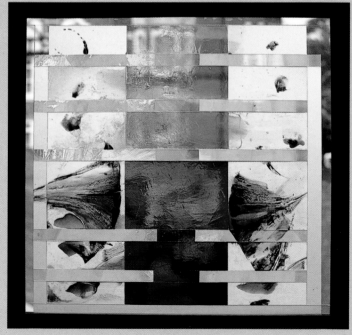

Autonomous panel, 1987 (left)
This panel, laminated between sheets of float glass, measures 20 x 20 feet (50 x 50cm) and is made in brown and opalescent antique glass, with acid-etching and fired enamels. The result is cool, structured and centered. The impingement of different materials, without the physical interruption and inevitable graphic structure of lead lines, emphasizes the various textures, allowing the purity of the abstract composition to emerge.

Stockley Park, Heathrow, England, 1986 (above, left and right)

Beleschenko won the shortlisted competition against two other artists for this stairwell window. The architects, Arup Associates, initially skeptical about working with a stained glass artist, later admitted their preconceptions had been based on an underestimation of the medium and its practitioners. The outstanding feature of the work is its complete absence of lead. Essentially, it is a suspended mosaic (see detail, right) in which thousands of pieces of antique glass are simply resting between two layers of toughened float glass. Every edge has been polished so that it properly abuts its neighbour and no chink of white light appears. Despite the fact that mouth-blown glass is far from constant in thickness, no resin or glue holds the pieces in place. The technical problems presented by this innovative technique were resolved by the artist in collaboration with the Derix Studio, which executed the window. With a lightness that assimilates it into the fabric of the building, the window is seductively soft in its message, and purposefully reveals the landscaped gardens beyond.

Essex County Council Building, Chelmsford, England, 1988 (this page and opposite)
Resulting from a competition with a painter, a sculptor and a tapestry maker, this commission was seen from the outset as a glass sculpture rather than as window glazing. Suspended on both sides of two internal columns are angled glass "sails." These appear like hanging banners, but have all the kinetic qualities of stained glass. The colourfulness of the work shows another facet of the artist's response to architecture. Careful resolution of technical problems (primarily the elimination of vertical outer frames which we would expect to be necessary as a means of support) have enabled the glass mosaics to achieve the appearance of floating in mid-air. Again, Beleschenko has achieved a striking sense of weightlessness through skilful exploitation of materials.

GRAHAM JONES

Graham Jones
Born, Warwickshire, England,
1958
*Studied at Lancaster Polytechnic
Art College, 1975-7. Studied
stained glass at the Swansea
College of Art, 1977-80. Received
the Howard Martin Design Award,
1980. Subsequently has
undertaken major commissions
in London for Shell UK and ICI.*

Graham Jones has only been designing stained glass
professionally since 1985, but already he has built up an
impressive portfolio of work and is clearly developing a
distinctive, colourful and emotive style.

He has shown a capacity to work in a variety of contexts,
within very restricted and relatively open briefs, finding
solutions to quite different problems relating to budget, the
client's special requirements and different styles of
architecture. Although the works shown here are strong in
coloration, his most current project is a glass sculpture
entirely made up of clear and opalescent antique glasses
etched and painted, and bolted to clear float glass.

He differs from many contemporary artists working in a
non-figurative style in that painting on glass is fundamental
to his approach. It is in the painting that he is able to capture
the latent imagery that is so often present in his work.
Sometimes he uses simple drapery to provide texture and
depth. More often, however, it is nature, in a primal sense,
that lurks behind the abstracted forms and contrasting
colours — landscapes, horizons, rocks, waves, fire, wind.

Basement corridor, Shell-Mex
Building, London, 1987
(left and right)
*This is an outstanding example of
a simple solution to an interior
design problem. In this space
originally were windows that
looked out onto two light-wells.
The artist was asked to design
something that would emphasize
the columns and the arches, be
relatively plain and
monochromatic, and be
achievable on a very small budget.
Each window has an outer
surround in plain sandblasted
glass, a narrow inner surround of
milk glass, and a central panel of
specially blown deep red opak. The
diameter of the circle at the top of
each window is very slightly
greater than the width of the red
pillar beneath: this has the effect
of emphasizing the arches and at
the same time of revealing all the
subtly different black grain lines
in the glass circles.*

Restaurant, Shell-Mex Building, London, 1987 (right and above)
These panels – a series of seven almost identical designs – are an original response to a common situation. The previous windows of the basement restaurant looked onto a dark alley, with a view mainly of brick walls and railings. Jones' backlit panels made it possible to retain the existing windows. The panels are partially lit by daylight, reinforced by powerful uplighters and small side spots that lend sparkle to the many glass prisms. An eye-level "horizon" of silhouetted low hills with brooding sky above gives a sense of depth to the basement space, while the prisms create a brilliant sharpness contrasting with the painted drapery below.

Shell-Mex building, London, 1989

A corridor with six arched window openings on each side makes a suitable site for a series of twelve panels, three of which are shown here. Because the arches are recessed, it is almost impossible to see more than two individual windows at once. Thus, the work is never experienced as an entirety — only as an unfolding narrative as you walk past. This visual separation of the panels has enabled the artist to be much bolder, and to create a sensation of walking through a radically changing spectrum of colour. As with the ICI windows (opposite), there is a sculptural tension in the designs. The use of paint is active and vehement, with a true sense of spontaneity. At the same time, the paint creates the moulding and contours which give these abstract forms their sense of depth, weight and movement.

ICI building, Millbank, London, 1988 (above and overleaf)
When renovating the superb 1920s building, the architects came up against these marble window frames that in the new plan for the office complex would have offered no exterior view. Rather than lose this distinctive feature of the staircase, ICI commissioned Graham Jones to design a series of seven backlit panels, as part of its new collection of contemporary art. The panels aim to capture the stylistic transition that characterizes the new complex — 1920s classical architecture blending into 1980s modernity. A primary inspiration was the Hungarian Constructivist painter László Moholy-Nagy, whose work was contemporary with the original building. The panels are
(Continued overleaf)

(Continued from page 133)

seen mainly obliquely, from either above or below, as you climb the spiralling staircase; at some levels they are visible through the marble arches from the lift landings (near left, top and bottom). The designs are based around a series of right-angled fulcrum points, each at a different position in the rectangle, moving upward as you ascend. On the lower floors blue and green predominate, moving into yellows and reds at higher levels of the building. Although the work is designed as a series, each panel works in its own right. There is a finely tuned balance of geometry and weight of colour — the smallest alteration would upset this equilibrium, tipping a panel forward or backward. These are invigorating works, full of dynamic arrested movement, symphonic in their overall sense of unity.

PRACTICALITIES

The text that follows deals with some aspects of commissioning stained glass; it is intended to be of use to architects and patrons, both public and private.

Creating a brief

Stained glass commissions stem from a number of possible sources. Residential commissions normally come from the imagination and interests of the houseowner, but they can frequently reflect the vision of an interior designer. Commissions in public buildings are most often inspired by architects or design companies, although sometimes the initial concept is provided by the owner of the building, the property developer or a public body that sponsors art in architecture.

Regardless of the initiator of the proposal, it is always important to attempt to define your own objectives clearly before talking to studio or artist or to an art consultant. It is important to decide what the stained glass is there to achieve — both on a practical and an aesthetic level.

For example, the stained glass may have some functional purpose, such as obscuring an ugly outlook, utilizing bricked-up window frames, or enclosing or enhancing a space. There may also be certain "commercial" objectives — to attract visitors, to make an environment more welcoming, to create an ambience that will make people want to stay longer, and so on. The stained glass might be planned as a modest decoration that is responsive to the architecture, or it might be perceived as a *pièce de résistance*, a focal point — Art with a capital "A".

Such objectives are not mutually exclusive. In practice, they may combine, creating parameters that help to determine (a) the choice of designer for the glass, and (b) the brief to be given to the artist.

Choosing a studio or artist

In stained glass there is a distinction to be made, although not a very exact one, between studios and artists. This distinction is particularly pronounced in Germany, although in recent years more and more British and American artists have started working with larger studios.

Most artists in stained glass can make their own stained glass panels, and many will do so unless the commission is large and they need to work with a studio to have the project completed within a reasonable length of time. However, there are a number of artists, some of whom are extremely knowledgeable about stained glass and excellent craftsmen, who perceive themselves primarily as designers, and so rarely execute their own designs. There have also been painters, notably Marc Chagall and John Piper, who have made a speciality of designing stained glass executed by specialist craftsmen.

When contemplating a project of any size or sophistication, there are definite benefits, not least financial ones, in having the skills, resources and wide experience of a large studio available.

There are stained glass studios of every size throughout the world, and most can offer excellent results. Most studios, large or small, will have their own "house" designer. He or she acts somewhat like a commercial artist, and will often be able to produce a design in almost any chosen style. The house designer will be knowledgeable about the medium and, if experienced, about its history. A studio artist can often make a design to reflect any historical period, or in any style you might desire, as well as being able to create an original piece in a modern idiom.

It is also possible to commission a design from an ordinary illustrator, or even from your own imagination, and then to consult a studio about making a window from that design. Such designs will often need to be converted into a form suitable for glass, but a good studio will in most cases be able to do this quite satisfactorily.

For the average residential project the architect or patron really needs to shop around locally, ask a number of studios to send a brochure, or, much more productive, visit a studio and see its portfolio.

Anyone contemplating a major commission should consider seeking early advice on the probable overall costs, the practical problems relating to the specific context, and the artists who might be appropriate for such a commission.

There are three ways to gain this sort of advice. One is to go to a large studio, especially a studio that specializes in working for artists. There you can be advised on all the practical considerations and at the same time you will be provided with an unbiased review of the work of a wide variety of artists who might be suitable for the job.

The second option, if available, is to consult the files of a craft organization or other public body that keeps a slide collection of a wide variety of stained glass artists. Such institutions often have extensive lists but often are not able to make personal recommendations, as they are intended to provide impartial information to the public.

Finally, you could seek out a commercial art consultant who keeps files on stained glass artists. He or she can show you the works of a number of different artists and introduce you to one or more suitable candidates, without your having to make any commitment.

As with most choices of this kind, the final decision is frequently made on very subjective grounds. Sometimes the designing of a stained glass window is very much a collaborative affair, with input from the architect and the client as well as the artist. It is often the sense that it would be enjoyable and productive to enter this sort of relationship with a particular artist that determines who receives the commission.

Competitions

As with architectural commissions, an approach often taken in stained glass is to hold a competition to decide on the artist. These competitions are normally short-listed between two, three or four artists after a preliminary selection process; but sometimes they are open to all.

Any short-listed competition should be on the basis of a fee guaranteed to all entrants. In my experience these fees seldom cover the costs of visits to the site, attendance at various meetings and at the presentation itself, and the physical preparation of the artwork — leaving aside the time in designing. In fact, competition fees seem in many cases to be derisory.

It would be welcome to see "rejection fees," as they are sometimes called, more commensurate with the expense and labour involved.

It is easy to underestimate the time it can take to design a stained glass window. The possibilities are infinite, and just to present one design can take a considerable length of time. It is easy, when looking at a final presentation, to fail to appreciate the lengthy process of experimentation and rejection that can be involved in achieving that single end-product.

This is one of the reasons that a number of more established artists will not enter competitions at all. Design competitions are often, in reality, not so much about establishing the actual design of the window: they are about deciding which artist to work *with*. An established artist will often find it unnecessary to go through this process to obtain satisfactory commissions.

Despite these factors, competitions can be very valuable. For one thing, they are often the route by which younger artists establish themselves. Secondly, a client may have no idea at all of what he wants, and a competition may help to crystallize his feelings, generating a whole variety of ideas, all of which may be useful in determining the end-result.

Craftsmanship

It is not possible to convey adequately in a few short paragraphs what are the qualities of the superb craftsman and the shortcomings of the inferior craftsman.

The good craftsman will handle lead with a dexterity and a neatness that come only with experience and with the unwavering pursuit of high standards. The glass will be cut with great accuracy, preventing aesthetic errors and ensuring maximum airtightness and sturdiness of the window. The soldering will be sound, but unobtrusive. Finally, the handling of the technical problems to do with installation, reinforcement of the window and so on, will result in a piece that is simple to install and long-lasting, without posing any long-term maintenance problems.

Interpretation of another artist's design requires a special understanding of the medium, great technical ability and a sensitivity to the artist's requirements. All these aspects constitute a specialist talent in itself.

The cost of stained glass

The major costs in the production of a stained glass window are: (a) the design, (b) the preparation of templates, or site measurements, (c) the preparation of a full-size cartoon, (d) the glass, (e) the fabrication, (f) the frames, (g) insurance and transportation to site, (h) installation.

(a) Design

The fee for a window design can vary widely, depending on the scale of the project and many other factors. If I can venture a generalization, the fees for stained glass design, even for well-known artists at the peak of their careers, are extremely low when compared, for example, to the prices paid for paintings. Obviously, some artists charge more than others. If you are lucky, you may find a very talented designer at the start of his career: with a reputation not yet made, the artist may be in no position to levy a high fee. As with painting, the discerning buyer can spot talent that is as yet unrecognized, and can reap the rewards.

(b) Glass

Most glass that is used in stained glass projects is expensive. Once you start to cut up the glass, you create wastage of the material — so that a window of only 3 square feet (1 sq m) may easily require the purchase of double that amount of glass. Not all colours cost the same amount. Flash glass costs more than regular antique. Machine-rolled glass costs about a quarter the price of antique, and float glass costs even less. The material costs are often about a third of the overall cost of making the stained glass.

(c) Fabrication

The fabrication of stained glass — cutting, painting, acid-etching, firing, leading, soldering and cementing — is a labour-intensive activity. The number of pieces of glass in each square yard or square meter will have a great impact on the cost of a window. A window with many small pieces of glass will be considerably more expensive than a window with only a few pieces. Even the smallest amount of painting or etching will add significantly to the cost, as both these processes are very time-consuming and require highly skilled labour. Many contemporary windows, even seemingly complex ones, are made without painting on the glass at all — not so much because of budgetary considerations, but more in response to the nature of contemporary design. A clean, stark idiom is not necessarily sympathetic to the more painterly effects of brushwork.

(d) Frames

Frames are discussed in more detail later. The costs can vary enormously. Often, the responsibility for the frames will remain with the architect who may consult with the studio and the artist only on technical and aesthetic aspects. Most stained glass artists, because they have no financial interest in the making of the frames, will tend to organize functional, plain, inexpensive framing. But I have known windows where the frames, specified by the architect, cost as much or more than the stained glass. This seems absurd, but real value is never easily quantified!

(e) Transporting to site

This is basically inexpensive, although the packing requires experience and care, and should always be done thoroughly. The product should, of course, be insured during transit.

(f) Installation

The installation of stained glass is not essentially dissimilar from the installation of any other type of glazing. The cost of installation depends upon the time taken, which largely depends upon the context and design of the frames. Internal panels and ceiling lights, which do not have to be airtight, are normally "sealed" with a self-adhesive neoprene padding, and are simple and quick to install. External panels require sealing around the edges, which is normally done with putty. This takes significantly longer and will cost more.

Conclusion

In general terms you can pay a great deal for stained glass or relatively little. There are windows illustrated in this book that cost ten times as much as other windows, though this may not necessarily reflect the quality or impact of the work. Some of the most successful works shown in the book were designed to a restricted budget — the artist found a solution to the problem by juggling with the materials and the design to achieve a simple yet effective result.

Framing

The basic design requirements of a framing system for stained glass are little different from those of any ordinary glazing frame. A rebate is required for the panel to push against, and some form of beading to hold the panel in place. The thickness of the lead border of a panel is normally ⅜in/9mm. The space that should be allowed for the glazing, including putty is ½in/12mm. In a standard wood frame a depth of ⅜in-⅝in/10-15mm is sufficient for the rebate.

If the panel is to be internal and does not require to be especially watertight, a packing of self-adhesive neoprene foam will frequently be used. If the panel is to be external, putty or silicone is normally used, although some rubber seal systems have sufficient flexibility to seal the many minor bumps that are caused by the nature of lead came itself, and by the soldered joints.

Frames can be made from various materials, depending on the nature of the building. They are frequently ordinary wood frames, sealed only with putty or with putty and a wood bead. They can be made in mild or stainless steel, brass or aluminium/aluminum, with screwed-in matching metal beading.

An effective but simple system for internal screens involves two 1 x ³⁄₁₆in/25 x 5mm wide flat steel bars, ⅜in/10mm apart. The bars are drilled with matching holes and connected together at regular intervals by a nut and bolt system. The stained glass panels rest on the threaded bolts at the bottom, and are retained on the other three sides by a similar system of bolts.

Existing double glazing

In many modern buildings, stained glass is installed inside existing double glazing. If the existing frame has sufficient depth, this can be done very simply by attaching metal beads with self-tapping screws to the inner edges of the existing frame and installing the panels in between. If there is not sufficient depth in the existing frame, then an additional frame must be attached to its face. Either way, the gap between the stained glass and the double glazed units must be at least 1in/25mm. There MUST be vent apertures created at top and bottom to allow the circulation of air between the two layers of glass.

Secondary glazing

If secondary glazing is planned (see below), the frame rebate needs to be wider, up to 1½in/40mm, excluding the beading, to allow for the stained glass itself (⅓in/9mm), the spacer (1in/25mm) and the secondary glazing (⅛-¼in/3-6mm).

Ceilings

Most ceiling panels are simply internal suspended systems. The glass rests in a simple T-section frame, very similar to that of any other suspended ceiling system. Each panel can be simply pushed up in order to change light bulbs behind, remove any dust that has settled, and so on.

External ceiling panels are more complicated. Water can easily get trapped by the lead into little puddles, which will start to decay the glass, the lead and the putty seal (see below, under Maintenance). For this reason most external ceiling lights have external secondary glazing, or are laminated with a resin-based laminate, or are sealed into double-glazed units (see below).

Designing a frame

In planning the framing of a large installation, several factors are at work. The silhouette of the frame may be designed by the artist in a way that works best with the window design. Often a very simple grid structure works best. The more regular the structure, the more the eye tends to ignore the interruptions and see only the design.

The major consideration in planning a frame is support for the glass. Stained glass panels, particularly when made with lead as is most common, are extremely flexible. This has several advantages but requires that the frames provide considerable support.

Most stained glass windows are built up of a series of individual panels. In a rectangular panel, the longest side should not be much more than 5ft/1.5m; the total area should not be more than 15 sq ft/1.5 sq m. It is quite possible to make panels larger, but the inconvenience of handling larger sizes during making, packing, shipping and installation often outweighs the advantages.

Because of the natural flexibility of lead, a stained glass panel has little innate rigidity. Unsupported, it will tend to sag and bow, responding to gravity. Because of this basic flexibility, panels require care in handling. They should never be picked up horizontally because they are capable of literally folding in half. When installed vertically, panels need to be securely supported by the frame to prevent the possibility of their sagging into a concertina-like shape. This effect can be quite often seen in old church windows; usually it happens because the original support system has decayed and is no longer working.

To ensure that panels do not sag or bow, regularly spaced reinforcing bars, normally made of zinc or mild steel (approximately ⅛ x ½in/3 x 12mm) or of circular brass rods, are soldered or "tied" to the rear of the glass, and rebated into the frame. They are fixed to the glass horizontally, appearing as a straight bar across the design. Alternatively, they can be curved to follow lead lines in the design, and thus be entirely disguised.

Weight of glass
Stained glass panels weigh anything from 30-60lb per square yard (15-30kg per sq m), depending upon the amount of lead used in a design. Weight is an important consideration when designing a framing system and planning a load factor.

Secondary/protective glazing
Secondary glazing is frequently added to existing or new stained glass as protection from: (a) decay caused by atmospheric pollution, (b) accidental damage (eg from hailstorms) or vandalism, (c) heat loss from lack of insulation.

Normally, secondary glazing takes the form of a sheet of clear glass, which can be laminated or toughened if required, that is placed outside the stained glass. It is separated from the stained glass by not less than 1in/25mm, a and is *not* a sealed unit.

Protective glazing can also be made from plastic, although plastic has several disadvantages. It tends to become abraided and eventually lose its transparency, and is easily scratched. Moreover, it will sag or bow, and in one case I know bowed inward so much that it started to push against the stained glass and eventually cracked a piece. Of the various plastics available, polycarbonates normally perform best, as well as having better fire rating specifications.

Occasionally, the secondary glazing is placed on the inside (see the Regensburg project, page 41). This allows the sculptural quality of the leadwork to be emphasized, and protects the stained glass from accidental damage from the inside. External secondary glazing will make the stained glass behind almost invisible from the outside in daylight: all that will be seen is reflections off the plain glass.

Secondary glazing can be added to the stained glass panels during fabrication, or it can be part of the installation. However it is installed, it is crucial that a current of air is able to pass through the space between the two layers of glass. This is sometimes achieved by drilling small holes at the top and bottom of the frame, between the two layers of glass. Ideally, the venting will be to the interior of the building, allowing a relatively warm dry current of air to pass between the panels.

In many churches, the secondary glazing occupies the original stone rebate and stained glass panels are literally suspended about 2in/5cm in front of the exterior glass. Vent holes that have been manufactured in the supporting spacer allow air to pass freely between the layers.

If vent holes are not provided, moisture will be trapped inside the space. The effects of this are described below.

The value of secondary glazing, and its possible dangers, are not always clearly understood. It will solve some problems, and help with others, but has the potential to be harmful, if done incorrectly or in the wrong context.

On the whole, it is only medieval glass that suffers from the damaging effects of atmospheric acids. Lead is safe from decay caused by pollution. Putty decays, regardless of any protection, at a relatively predictable rate — its lifespan is normally 75-100 years.

With old stained glass whose putty has decayed, heat loss may be quite severe, but secondary glazing, which cannot be sealed and *must* be vented, cannot prevent this. Only restoration of the putty will deal with this problem.

The greatest enemy of stained glass is water. Standing water or moisture etches glass, removes paint, corrodes lead and metal frames, rots wood, and decays mortar from stone. Protective glazing can, if not properly vented, cause more water or moisture damage than anything the atmosphere can bring to bear. Condensation can build up between the two panels and fail to evaporate; this retained moisture will start to dissolve the glass and corrode the lead and metal support bars.

Leaded windows are never totally airtight: air and moisture will always penetrate leaded joints.

Finally, it is worth bearing in mind that old buildings can suffer from being suddenly sealed — interior wood, fabrics, and other artefacts, particularly organ pipes in churches, may respond very poorly to a sudden reduction of humidity and of air circulation.

When planning secondary glazing, the important considerations are:
1) Should it be plain, toughened or laminated glass, or a light plastic?
2) Should it be placed inside or outside?
3) Can it be easily removed and maintained?
4) Is the air circulation sufficient to prevent condensation or moisture build-up?
5) Is it responsive to the aesthetics of the building?

Double-glazed units
It is possible to incorporate stained glass panels into double glazed units. The advantages are:
(a) The enormous ease of cleaning,
(b) Complete thermal protection and insulation,

(c) Potential protection on both sides from damage.
The disadvantages are:
(a) The additional cost, which is not great,
(b) The increased weight and thickness of the panels,
(c) The loss of surface texture, and the reflections that appear in the glass and can hide the image within. This problem can be solved, of course, using non-reflective glass, but this is not available as a toughened glass, and only in a new and very expensive product as laminated glass.

With a spacer bar of at least ½ inch (1.2cm), the panels obviously become quite thick — ¾ inch (20mm) or more — and heavy. It is important that the panel inside is securely positioned so that it cannot start to tilt and touch one of the two enclosing glass panes. Also, the panel must not be so large that it starts to bow inside the double glazing, with the danger that its center will touch the external glass. This can be avoided by inserting invisible, non-conducting, clear plastic spacers into the lead in the center of the panel.

If a double-glazed panel is exposed to intense sunlight, the whole panel can heat up inside, possibly to the point where glass fractures. This is especially possible if the glass inside is dark in colour or relatively opaque. Windows that face the sun will be especially prone to this sort of heat build-up, and should not be double-glazed.

Lighting

The artificial lighting of stained glass is not an exact science. Some lighting designers have begun to make a speciality of it, but it is hard to find one with extensive experience.

Backlighting

Fluorescent tubes are most commonly used to backlight stained glass. If these are placed directly behind the glass, some form of diffusion screen is required to spread the light: this is normally plastic, which is very lightweight, but sandblasted glass can be used. After a stained glass panel has been leaded *and* puttied, it is possible to lightly sandblast the whole reverse side. This treatment needn't damage the lead, and will act as a light diffuser.

Often, tube lights are positioned parallel to the edges of the panel, as this causes minimum interference to the design by variations in light intensity. Preferably, the tubes are placed facing the back wall, which should be white or otherwise reflective: the light bounces off the rear surface to illuminate the panels.

In my experience, the optimum lights are metal halide uplighters. An occasional difficulty with these lights is that the tiniest variation in the manufacturing process can lead them to give off slightly distorted colours. Hence, a bank of lights may all have slight colour variations. However, generally speaking, the light given off is the closest to daylight possible. Halogen lights, being essentially yellow, result in distortions in the colours of the glass.

Some backlit panels benefit from a curved plaster wall behind. This allows the spread of light to be evened out over the whole area. Otherwise reflectors can be built from computer-calculated specifications that will cast the light in a precise curve to provide uniform lighting, even over a curved or vaulted surface.

Positioning lighting so that it cannot be seen through the glass allows the artist considerably more freedom. He is not restricted in his design to opaque glass, and can thus play with depths and contrasts that are not always possible if the panel, or the diffusion screen behind it, has to hide the lighting.

In one backlit project I have been involved with we decided to use paint not only on the glass but also on the white rear wall behind the glass: this gave new possibilities of mobility to the work, as the rear design would move in relation to the foreground as you walked past the panels.

Night lighting

The exterior view at night is a crucial aspect of stained glass design in many public buildings. Ideally, the artificial lighting should try to wash across the glass, bringing out the highlights and the special texture of the antique glass. As is well demonstrated in the vaulted roof window at Buxton, Derbyshire, England (see pages 82-3), a controlled interior-positioned "wash" of light can enable the glass to be visible at night from outside, while retaining the colours when the glass is seen from inside. The view from inside at night will be distinct from the view in daylight, as the colours will be flattened; nonetheless, it will form an interesting variation in the appearance.

The one thing to avoid when lighting stained glass is mounting spotlights behind a window (that is, outside) in the hope that it will bring colour to the interior view at night: the only result will be small circular pools of light in the window. The light source must be diffused over the whole area, or lit from below or above.

Finally, there is front lighting. Strictly speaking, stained glass windows require a greater intensity of light behind the glass than in front. Many stained glass panels will become quite dead if the "surface" light is brighter than the light behind. However, it is possible to design panels specifically to be illuminated by a frontal light source.

There are many ways to achieve excellent effects in this context. Antique glass can be silvered, or mirror can be placed behind the panel. *Opak* glass will perform well when lit by surface light, as the opaque white flash reflects the light back through the colour. Hence, a sufficient recess for back-lighting internal stained glass is ideal but should not be considered mandatory.

The strength of stained glass

Even architects will sometimes question the robustness of stained glass, but a moment's thought will show that such worries are needless. Stained glass windows have been around a long time. They endure. At the same time they mature like wonderful antiques, developing ever greater richness with the passage of time.

Stained glass panels are remarkably strong. Recently in Cyprus a terrorist's bomb blew out all the windows for several hundred yards in all directions — except for some stained glass windows near the source of the explosion. The windows undulated gently as they absorbed the shockwaves, and only two small pieces cracked.

The main reason for the resistance of stained glass to damage is its flexibility. It can survive impact and shock that would shatter most ordinary glass. Even if a window is subjected to direct impact, often the only damage is the breaking of one small piece of glass, which can be easily repaired.

Stained glass is bonded together by lead and by putty. The one is elastic and absorbs shock, the other is a remarkably retentive adhesive. When repairing small broken pieces it is remarkable how difficult it can be to extract the shattered glass. The inside of lead is corrugated, creating an abraded surface to which putty binds. Thus, even when broken or shattered, most of the glass will tend to remain in place.

In 1986 York Minster, one of the great cathedrals of England, particularly noted for its stained glass, experienced a major fire. Although some windows were completely destroyed, no part of the lead or glass or even the solder actually landed on the floor below. The entire weblike structure remained bonded together, even though it was reduced to an almost indistinguishable pile of molten material.

The weak element in stained glass is the actual glass. And its greatest enemy, after water, is stress. If the glass is put under stress, either by being pressed upon too strongly, or twisted, or subjected to stresses from the movement of a building, it can fracture. For these reasons, the best installation methods try to reduce these possibilities, sealing the glass while still allowing some freedom of movement.

Maintenance

The quality of the original craftsmanship, and the design and planning of the installation, determine the longevity of stained glass.

Every one hundred years or so, the putty will need attention. This will probably involve taking the entire window apart and releading it, although it is possible to make some temporary improvement to decayed putty without going through this process.

Basically, however, stained glass requires very little maintenance. Unlike float glass it does not need cleaning on a monthly basis because the accumulation of dirt is not readily visible in the same way — a factor that should be considered in calculating its long-term cost.

Useful Addresses

Australia
The Crafts Council of Australia
100 George Street
Sydney, New South Wales 2000
(02) 241-1701

Canada
Canadian Crafts Council
46 Elgin Street, Suite 16
Ottawa K1P 5K6
(613) 235-8200

Artists in Stained Glass (AISG)
Canada
c/o Ontario Crafts Council
35 McCaul Street
Toronto M5T 1V7
(416) 977-3511

Canadian Clay & Glass Gallery
25 Caroline Street North
Waterloo
Ontario N20 2Y5
(519) 746 1882

Great Britain
British Society of Master Glass
Painters
6 Queen Square
London WC1
(0171) 883 0348

The Crafts Council
44a Pentonville Road
London N1 9BY
(0171) 278 7700

Worshipful Company of
Glaziers
Glaziers Hall
9 Montague Close
London SE1 9DD

Andrew Moor Associates
(consultant)
14 Chamberlain Street
London NW1 8XB
(0171) 586 8181

Denmark
Glasmuseum
Strandvejen 8
DK – Ebeltoft

France
Int. Nat. du Nouvel
Objet Visuel
27 Rue de l'Université
F 75007 Paris

Centre International du Vitrail
5 rue de Cardinal Pie
F 2800 Chartres

Spain
Districta de l'Eixamplo
Ajunctament de Barcelona
Casa Elizaldo
Valencia, 302

Japan
Crafts Council of Japan
#503 Yoyogi 4-28-28
Shibuya-Ku,
Tokyo 151

New Zealand
Crafts Council of New Zealand
22 The Terrace
PO Box 498
Wellington 1
(044) 727-018

NZ Society of Artists in Glass
c/o Peter Raos
2a Bulwer Street
Devonport
Auckland

United States
The Census of Stained Glass
(magazine)
PO Box 1531
Raleigh, NC 27602
(215) 683-7341

The Corning Glass Museum
1 Museum Way
Corning, NY 14830
(607) 937-5371

American Crafts Council
40 West 53rd Street
New York, NY 10019
(212) 956-3535

The Glass Art Society Inc.
PO Box 1364
Corning,
NY 14830
(607) 936-0530

The Stained Glass Association of
America
4050 Broadway, Suite 219
Kansas City, MO 64111
(816) 561-4404

West Germany
Hessisches Landesmuseum
Friedensplatz 1
6100 Darmstadt

Kunstmuseum
Ehrenhof 5
4000 Düsseldorf

Galerie Derix
Platterstrasse 94
D 6204 Taunusstein
(061 28) 84201

Neues Glas/New Glass
(magazine, quarterly, in English
and German)
Verlagsanstalt Handwak Gmbh
Postfach 8120
D4000 Düsseldorf 1
(0211) 30 70 73

GLOSSARY

Pages on which types of glass are illustrated and more fully explained are given in brackets after an entry. Cross-references are in SMALL CAPITALS.

Acid-etching The process of working into the surface of glass using acid. This technique is particularly used to cut through FLASHED colour.

American opalescent A ROLLED GLASS, invented by L.C. Tiffany in the 1870s, that is largely a mixture of wispy colours on a white base. Sometimes simply called "opalescent." (10)

Antique glass Sheet glass made by the ancient mouth-blown process, with all the striations and texture that this process produces.

Beading The strip of material that is fixed to the frame after the glass has been inserted, keeping the glass pressed against the rebate. Normally, beading is made of the same material as the frame itself.

Bevels Polished angles cut into the edges of glass. (10)

Brilliant-cutting The process of grinding bevelled edges, circles, Vs and so on, into the surface of glass with a series of abrasive stones. (10)

Came The metal, I-shaped in profile, that is used to bond pieces of glass together. Came is usually lead, but can also be zinc or brass.

Cathedral glass The most common type of ROLLED coloured glass. It has a distinctive patterned texture to its surface, and comes in a limited range of colours. (10)

Constructivist A generic design term, based on the 1920s artistic movement, indicating a geometric, rectilinear style.

Copper foil A technique of bonding glass together that is widely used for decorative items such as lampshades. It allows for a more sculpted finish than lead, but does not have its strength.

Dalle de verre A technique whereby chunks of coloured glass ("slab glass") are bonded together with cement or epoxy. This type of glass has been extensively used since the 1950s.

Danziger A German name for a type of water glass, similar to English reamy glass. It has a flowing, watery surface texture.

Enamels The various coloured enamels used to paint onto glass.

Firing The process of firing paint or enamel onto the glass in a kiln. Firing of most vitreous enamals is done at around 1200-1250°F (650-680°C).

Flash glass Glass that has a skin of a different colour "flashed" onto the base glass, which is most often clear. (10)

Float glass Sheet glass manufactured according to the Pilkington patented method of floating liquid glass on molten tin.

Fusing Melting different colours of glass together in a kiln at temperatures around 1400°F (760°C).

Grisaille A technique, common from the 12th century on, of painting simple patterns in black on clear or white glass.

Laminated glass Two layers of glass bonded together by a resin. Sometimes called "safety glass," it is resistant to breakage or shattering — and difficult to cut.

Lead came The lead I-profile material used to join leaded glass. It comes in many different widths from ⅛ to 2¾in (3-70mm).

Lenses Circular "eyes" made in various sizes in cast glass. Lenses are quite often used in stained glass as decorative features.

Lusters Iridescent metallic colours that are used as decoration in ceramics and sometimes used in stained glass.

Matting The generic term for creating shaded tones with a brush and paint on glass; usually done after tracing.

Mouth-blown glass Glass that is made by blowing molten glass into a "muff" (bubble).

Opak Clear or coloured ANTIQUE GLASS that has been FLASHED with an opaque white flash. (10)

Opal Clear or coloured ANTIQUE GLASS that has been flashed with a transparent opal or pearl finish. (10)

Opalescent A clear ANTIQUE GLASS with an opal flash. Opalescent can come in a variety of different tones of white. (10) (See also AMERICAN OPALESCENT)

Opaque A descriptive word often used in stained glass to mean "not transparent"; it does not mean "not translucent."

Paint The term is used mainly to describe the black/brown vitreous enamel used for TRACING and MATTING on glass. These paints contain the same elements as glass and are fired at temperatures of 1200-1250°F (650-680°C).

Plating Putting two pieces of glass into one LEAD CAME. This is normally done to achieve subtle colour, or to make repairs.

Prisms Pyramid-shaped cast BEVELS that are quite frequently used as decorative features in windows.

Reamy glass The common English term for an ANTIQUE GLASS with a flowing, watery surface texture. The term is virtually synonymous with *danziger* glass.

Resist A material that is used to cover selected areas of glass to mask them from either acid or SANDBLASTING.

Ribbed glass A fairly common type of ROLLED clear glass that has a series of parallel ribs approximately ½in (10mm) apart.

Rolled glass Glass that is made by passing molten glass through two parallel rollers. (10)

Rondels Spun "crowns" of glass, resembling plates. They can be specially made with interweaving colours.

Sandblasting A treatment whereby sand, projected by compressed air, abrades the surface of the glass. Sandblasting can penetrate the glass deeply and even be used to cut glass.

Seedy glass A type of ANTIQUE GLASS incorporating randomly scattered bubbles of many different sizes. (9)

Silverstain A silver oxide that provides a unique method of colouring glass. During firing, the stain penetrates deeply into the glass and is transparent. It produces shades of yellow.

Slab glass The glass used for making DALLE DE VERRE.

Slumping The process of bending glass on a mould at temperatures of more than 1000°F (540°C).

Solder The mixture of tin and lead (either 60:40 or 50:50) used to bond LEAD CAME together.

Spacer An aluminium/aluminum bar, available in many different widths, that is commonly used in double-glazing.

Tiffany glass A type of ROLLED GLASS: see AMERICAN OPALESCENT. Most is still made in America.

Toughened glass Otherwise termed "tempered glass." The term refers to glass that has been heated and rapidly cooled, making it extremely strong.

Tracing The painting of outlines on glass, as distinct from the shaded effects produced by MATTING.

Zinc came A type of CAME sometimes used, particularly in America, as an alternative to lead. It is more rigid than lead.

INDEX

PICTURE CREDITS